MONSTERS OF NEW JERSEY

MONSTERS
OF NEW JERSEY

Mysterious Creatures in the Garden State

Loren Coleman and
Bruce G. Hallenbeck

STACKPOLE
BOOKS

Published by
STACKPOLE BOOKS
5067 Ritter Road
Mechanicsburg, PA 17055
www.stackpolebooks.com

Portions of this book are based in small part on the following previously published material by Loren Coleman: "Winged Weirdies," *FATE*, March 1972, with Jerome Clark; Chapters 6 and 7 from *Creatures of the Outer Edge* with Jerome Clark (New York: Warner, 1978; New York: Anomalist Books, 2006); Chapter 8 of *Curious Encounters* (Boston: Faber and Faber, 1985); "On the Trail," *Fortean Times*, January and May 1997 and March 1998; "Mysterious World," *FATE*, July 1999; Chapter 18 and marginal material from *Mysterious America* (New York: Simon and Schuster, 2006); and Cryptomundo.com postings, 2006–2010. Kind permission has been granted by Mark A. Hall to reproduce material on the "Wooo-wooo" from his *Thunderbirds!* (Bloomington, MN: Privately published, 1988) and by Laura K. Leuter, president of The Devil Hunters, for material to be found in the appendix.

Printed in the United States of America

10 9 8 7 6 5 4 3 2 1

FIRST EDITION

Cover art by Marc Radle
Cover design by Tessa J. Sweigert

Library of Congress Cataloging-in-Publication Data

Coleman, Loren.
Monsters of New Jersey : mysterious creatures in the Garden State / Loren Coleman and Bruce G. Hallenbeck. — 1st ed.
p. cm.
ISBN-13: 978-0-8117-3596-4 (pbk.)
ISBN-10: 0-8117-3596-6 (pbk.)
1. Cryptozoology—New Jersey. 2. Monsters—New Jersey. 3. Animals, Mythical—New Jersey. I. Hallenbeck, Bruce G., 1952- II. Title.
QL89.C647 2010
001.94409749—dc22

2010019431

To Jerry Dale Coleman, William Coleman, Susan Hoey,
and Martha Hallenbeck

"If I had a world of my own, everything would be non-sense. Nothing would be what it is because everything would be what it isn't. And contrary-wise; what it is it wouldn't be, and what it wouldn't be, it would. You see?"

—Lewis Carroll

Alice's Adventures in Wonderland

CONTENTS

INTRODUCTION

No Neat Little Pigeonholes

Charles Fort, that clever New York City researcher into matters inexplicable and author of such classic works as *The Book of the Damned*, once noted that excluded and damned data "arrange themselves in mass-formations that pass and pass and keep on passing."

Fort should know, as he was one of the earliest writers to try to tackle the slippery strangeness of the Jersey Devil. We shall see that New Jersey's special and lively cryptozoological Forteana, as the overall study of strange phenomena is now called in Charles Fort's honor, is not easy to place into neat little boxes. It is similar to trying to put water in a bucket full of holes; once you get it in, before you know it, it is someplace else.

New Jersey's monsters are very much like the water flowing from that hole-filled bucket. Of all the states in America, it appears this one has no neat little pigeonholes in which to conceptualize and organize the terrible creatures seen in the air above, the bizarre beasts encountered on the land below, and the mysterious monsters sighted in the waters off the Jersey shores.

Nevertheless, with our hands firmly on the steering wheel as we rush around the parkways and waterways of the state, we shall explore the woods, backyards, Pine Barrens, lakes, and sea where New Jersey's creepy critters and unclassified cryptids are reported in this unique bit of land. New Jersey, we have come to discover, is much more than a place to call home for all those people who commute to work in New York City or live and work in the Garden State. Lest we forget, New Jersey is the fabled home to many monsters.

A NOTE ON STYLE

Why are animal names sometimes capitalized, sometimes in lowercase, and sometimes in italics? The style used in this book follows the manual of style adopted by the International Society of Cryptozoology and its peer-reviewed scientific journal, *Cryptozoology*. The journal's editor, Richard Greenwell, detailed the proper capitalization of cryptozoological names, before and after discovery, in a footnote on page 101 of the 1986 issue of *Cryptozoology*. Greenwell followed the same manual of style used in systematic zoology.

Greenwell is very clear in his example:

> Native name: okapi;
> Western name for presumed, undiscovered animal:
> Okapi;
> Common name after discovery and acceptance:
> okapi.

For our extended use, this translates into the following form:

> Native name: nahuelito;
> Western name for presumed, undiscovered animal:
> Nahuelito;

Common name after discovery and acceptance:
nahuelito.

Native name: naitaka;
Western name for presumed, undiscovered animal:
Ogopogo;
Common name after discovery and acceptance:
ogopogo.

Therefore, as Lake Monster, Sea Serpent, and Nessie have not been technically "accepted" by systematic zoology as of this date, the capitalized form is employed in this book.

The Jersey Devil

The joke circulating in 2010 about the Jersey Devil goes something like this: If you live in New Jersey, get up in the morning, and pour milk on your cereal to only find the milk is sour, the Jersey Devil did it. If you then go out to your car, and find you have a flat tire, well, the Jersey Devil did it. If your hockey team loses in the playoffs, guess what . . . You get the idea.

So what is the Jersey Devil after all?

Today, in New Jersey, the umbrella term *Jersey Devil* seems to apply to anything that has a curse or bad luck associated with it. The Jersey Devil is one of those localized names that residents have applied to any supposed strange beast, entity, or phantom seen in the state. The legendary creature, in fact, is New Jersey's "official demon," a regional mascot, and the name of the state's National Hockey League team.

The Jersey Devil, as a feral human initially identified as a Bigfoot, was featured in the third episode of the TV series *The X-Files*, as the first ever "monster of the week." A 1990s Sony PlayStation game turned the savage beast into a likeable videogame character, and in this new century, the Jersey Devil has been a frequent topic of reality television programs. But the history of the beast is much older.

The first people to note the presence of a peculiar animal in the general area were the Native Americans, who said it originally appeared across state lines in what is now Bucks County, Pennsylvania (where alleged sightings of the Devil have been made in recent years), just north of Philadelphia. In fact, the local Indians named the creek Popuessing, meaning "place of the dragon."

In 1677, Swedish explorers examined some weird footprints in the rocks near the same creek and renamed it Drake Kill, which also refers to a dragon.

But the main locus has always been New Jersey, of course. The Jersey Devil, sometimes called the Leeds Devil, has been seen since the 1930s, but long before that a great body of folklore had grown up around the elusive beast. Some versions of the legend—folklorists claim there are more than thirty variants of the tale in circulation—list the creature's alleged birth as having taken place in 1887. The Gloucester Historical Society, however, has traced the tale back as far as 1790, and there is every reason to believe it was around even earlier.

The most frequently related account of the Devil's origins goes like this: In 1735, a Mrs. Leeds of Estellville, New Jersey, upon finding she was pregnant for the thirteenth time and less than exhilarated about it, snorted that if she was going to have another child it might just as well be a devil—and it was. It was born with an animal's head, a bird's body, and cloven hooves instead of feet. Cursing its mother (it could speak at birth, of course), it promptly flew up the chimney and took up residence in the swamps and Pine Barrens of southern New Jersey, where it has lived ever since. American folklore is filled with similar stories about a pregnant mother's careless words backfiring on her. As late as 1908, a tale circulating through rural Alabama had it that a Birmingham baby was born "with horns like a devil." During the pregnancy, the mother had remarked, "I'd as soon have a devil in the house as a baby!"

Over the years the story, like all good stories, grew in the telling. Eventually the Devil was held responsible for every major calamity that befell the state, and some people even maintained that its appearance presaged the coming of war. On a less cosmic scale it was said that its breath could sour milk, kill fish, and dry up cornfields.

The late Rev. Henry Carlton Beck recounted another part of the myth in his *Jersey Genesis*:

> Accompanied, as it usually is, by the howling of dogs and the hooting of owls, there can be no surer forerunner of disaster. Where the barrens line the shore it flits from one desolate grass-grown dune to another and is especially watchful upon those wild heights when coasting schooners, driving their prows into the sand, pound to splinters upon the bars and distribute upon the waves their freight of good and human lives.
>
> Upon such occasions Leeds' Devil is seen in the companionship of a beautiful golden-haired woman in white, or yet of some fierce-eyed, cutlass-bearing disembodied spirit of a buccaneer whose galleon, centuries ago, was wrecked upon the shore of Cape May County.

The legend claims that by the mid-1700s the Devil had become such a nuisance that a clergyman was called in to exorcise it. A century later, in 1840, a strange animal went on a rampage, slaughtering livestock, attempting to seize children, and generally terrorizing the area. In the course of one foray, it supposedly killed two large dogs, three geese, four cats, and thirty-one ducks. During the winter of 1873–74, the Devil was said to be seen prowling in the vicinity of Bridgeton;

in 1894–95, a trail of unidentifiable footprints around Leeds Point excited speculation that the beastie had returned to the place of its birth. Near Vincentown in 1899, farmers reported losing livestock to some kind of mystery animal.

Perhaps it was the same thing Mrs. Amanda Sutts saw on her family's farm in 1900. She recalled the incident for the Trenton *Evening Times* sixty years later, still convinced that the creature was the Jersey Devil. At the time of the incident, she was ten years old and living on a farm near Mays Landing in the heart of Devil country. Her story has become one of the classics of the field, well-worth sharing in some detail.

"We heard a scream near the barn one night and ran out of our house," she said. "We saw this thing that looked like a kangaroo. It wasn't such a great big animal—it was about the size of a small calf and weighed about 150 pounds. But the noise it made is what scared us. It sounded like a woman screaming in an awful lot of agony."

Mrs. Sutts said that was the only time she ever actually viewed the creature, but her family often heard it and would follow its tracks, which were eight to ten feet apart and led to a large cedar swamp at the rear of the farm. Her father had seen the thing once before, when he was sixteen years old.

"When the horses heard the Devil scream," she observed, "they would carry on so you'd think they were going to tear the barn down. You could hear the Devil scream a long way off when the horses would quiet down. People may say there's nothing to it but I know darned well there is. Some might say I'm an old crank but when you know a thing you know it."

So you begin to see the peculiar problem here. Perhaps this was a real cryptid, a mystery kangaroo, a devil monkey, or a Bigfoot? The screen of time influences the report on one level, but the location and overall lore of the Jersey Devil does even more so. Folklorists feel this is their domain, which surely it is, but the question has to be this: Are there any real animals underneath some of these stories from Jersey?

How seriously anyone took these yarns is hard to say, though some Jerseyites must have at least half believed them. Most people probably treasured the story of the origins of the Jersey Devil for its quaint and amusing character and kept it alive chiefly as a story used to entertain their children on Halloween.

Certainly New Jersey citizens, and others as well, have had their share of fun with the beast. In 1906 huckster Norman Jefferies, publicity manager for C. A. Brandenburgh's Arch Street Museum in Philadelphia, came upon an old book, which mentioned Mrs. Leeds's curious offspring, and it gave him an idea. With attendance at his shows declining, Jefferies had been on the lookout for a stunt to bring the crowds back. Unfortunately for him, the Philadelphia papers, having been taken in by earlier Jefferies tricks, were not about to offer him any cooperation. So he planted this story in a South Jersey small-town weekly:

> The "Jersey Devil," which has not been seen in these parts for nearly a hundred years, has again put in its appearance. Mrs. J. H. Hopkins, wife of a worthy farmer of our county, distinctly saw the creature near the barn on Saturday last and afterwards examined its tracks in the snow.

The report created a sensation. All over the state, men and women started glancing over their shoulders and bolting doors and windows. While always taking care publicly to profess skepticism, Jerseyites steadfastly refused to take any chances. What if the monster was real after all? Had not an "expert" from the Smithsonian Institution said that it "bore out his long cherished theory that there still existed in hidden caverns and caves, deep in the interior of the earth, survivors of those prehistoric animals and fossilized remains?" The expert was sure the Devil was a pterodactyl. Yes, a pterodactyl, said to have been extinct for more than 70 million years. At least.

Shortly thereafter the animal was captured by a group of farmers. After making sure every paper around got the news, Jefferies took the "Devil" with him to Philadelphia and placed it on exhibition in the Arch Street Museum. The crowds, huge and mostly uncritical, gazed in wonder at the thing—actually a kangaroo with bronze wings fastened to its back and green stripes painted the length of its body. Jefferies confessed in 1929 that he had bought the animal from a dealer in Buffalo, New York, and let it loose in a wooded area of South Jersey where it was certain to be caught without difficulty.

After Jefferies's hoax of 1906, things turned very serious a mere three years later. On a January night in 1909, E. P. Weeden of the City Council of Trenton, New Jersey, according to reports from that time, bolted upright in bed when he heard someone trying to break down his door. It was a most unusual "someone," apparently, because Weeden also heard distinctly the sound of flapping wings. Weeden rushed to his second-floor window and looked outside. He did not see the intruder, but the sight that greeted his eyes chilled him far more than the icy temperature ever could: something had left a line of tracks in the snow on the roof of his house. And whatever that "something" was, it had hooves.

On the same night, "it" left hoofprints in the snow at the State Arsenal in Trenton. Shortly afterwards, John Hartman of Centre Street caught a full view of it as it circled his yard and then vanished into the night. Trenton residents living near the Delaware River were shaken by loud screeching sounds, like the cries of a giant cat, and stayed in their homes that night too frightened to venture out.

"It" reappeared in Bristol, Pennsylvania, during the early morning hours of January 17. The first person to observe it, a police officer named Sackville, was patrolling along Buckley Street around 2:00 A.M. He was alerted by the barking of dogs in the neighborhood that something was amiss. Feeling increasingly uneasy, he reached a small bridge when a sudden movement from the path below caught his eye. Carefully, he turned his head. When he saw the creature, he was so stunned that, for a moment, he could not move.

Gathering his wits, Sackville drew his revolver and plunged toward it. The beast let out an eerie cry and hopped rapidly away, with the officer in hot pursuit. Suddenly it raised its wings and flew above the path, and Sackville, afraid that it would get away, fired his gun. He missed. By the time he got off a second shot, the thing was gone.

The second witness was Bristol postmaster E. W. Minster, who the next day told this story to reporters:

> I awoke about two o'clock in the morning . . . and finding myself unable to sleep, I arose and wet my head with cold water as a cure for insomnia.
>
> As I got up I heard an eerie, almost supernatural sound from the direction of the river. . . . I looked out upon the Delaware and saw flying diagonally across what appeared to be a large crane but which was emitting a glow like a firefly.
>
> Its head resembled that of a ram, with curled horns, and its long thin neck was thrust forward in flight. It had long thin wings and short legs, the front legs shorter than the hind. Again, it uttered its mournful and awful call—a combination of a squawk and a whistle, the beginning very high and piercing and ending very low and hoarse.

John McOwen, a liquor dealer who lived on Bath Street with the back of his house facing the Delaware Division Canal, heard his infant daughter crying and went into her room to see what was wrong. It was about 2:00 A.M. A "strange noise" brought him to the window, which overlooked the canal.

> It sounded like the scratching of a phonograph before the music begins . . . and yet it also had something of a whistle to it. You know how the factory whistle sounds? Well, it was something like that. I looked from the window and was astonished to see a large creature standing on the banks of the canal. It looked something like an eagle . . . and it hopped along the towpath.

The next day Mrs. Thomas Holland discovered hoofmarks in her snow-covered yard, as did other residents of Buckley and Bath streets. And Trenton and Bristol were not the only places where the creature was seen. At Camden, twelve men at work in the Hilltown clay bank took one glance at the thing as it descended toward them, and then, as one account wryly notes, they "were off to set an unofficial record for the three-mile run in working clothes."

Other New Jersey towns and cities reporting visitations were Wycombe, Swedesboro, Huffville, Mantua, Woodbury, Mount Ephraim, Haddonfield, and Mount Holly. Said a contemporary news story, "Hoofprints have been noticed in hundreds of places over a strip of country at least 16 miles long and three miles wide."

As the years went by, other incidents occurred. The Woodbury *Daily Times* got into the act, reporting in its December 15, 1925, issue that farmer William Hyman had killed an unknown animal after it raided his chicken coop. "Hyman describes the beast," the paper said, "as being as big as a grown Airedale with black fur resembling Astrakhan; having a kangaroo fashioned hop; forequarters higher than its rear, which were always crouched; and hind feet of four webbed toes."

Fine, except that "William Hyman" never existed. And neither, needless to say, did his specimen of the Jersey Devil.

But is there more to the Jersey Devil than mere folklore and fabrication? The question is certainly heretical enough. Even Charles Fort drew the line here, writing in *Lo!* that "though I should not like to be so dogmatic as to say there are no 'Jersey Devils,' I have had no encouragement investigating them." But Fort's knowledge of the phenomenon may have been confined to the Jefferies and Hyman hoaxes only.

The problem is complicated by the virtually absolute refusal of journalists to take the Devil at all seriously, even though some commentators have admitted rather uneasily that there are portions of the legend that are, well, odd—like the sterling characters of some of those individuals who insist they saw a mysterious thing with wings hopping or flying through the Pine Barrens, or the persistent discoveries of unusual tracks, or the unexplained disappearances of livestock, or the haunting cries sometimes heard emanating from the woods.

But reporters, perhaps understandably, would rather have the Devil be a charming, harmless piece of Halloween lore than an annoying puzzle for which there may be no ready answers. As a consequence, their treatment of even apparently authentic reports of unknown animals in New Jersey is almost invariably flippant, dotted with references to such obvious nonsense as Mrs. Leeds's baby, and ultimately confusing to anyone who endeavors to separate fact from fiction.

After the 1909 flap, the Devil went back into hiding, or so it would seem. In general, the Jersey Devil did not reappear in any big way again until June 1926, when two ten-year-old boys in West Orange reportedly saw what news accounts refer to vaguely as a "flying lion." A large posse scoured the area in search of the creature but found nothing.

Around August 1 of the following year, huckleberry pickers near Bridgeport startled an animal resting in a cedar swamp and chased it until it outdistanced them, hooting angrily all the while. A *New York Times* dispatch describes the animal "as large and as speedy as a fox and with four legs, but also having feathers and a cry that is partly bark and partly the hoot of an owl."

Almost exactly a year later, other berry pickers at Mays Landing and Leeds Point allegedly encountered a similar creature. Another witness was Mrs. William Sutton, a farmer's wife, who said she saw it in her cornfield. An unidentified man flagged down a car driven by Charles Mathis and pleaded that he needed to be taken from the scene of his meeting with "a horrible monster." A thirteen-year-old boy said he had seen the Devil gazing at him through his bedroom window.

In 1935, Philip Smith, "a sober gentleman of honest reputation," claimed he saw the Devil walking down a Woodstown street, and the next year, following an outbreak of alleged sightings, a posse of farmers searched neighboring forests and swamps without success.

It may be no more than a part of the legend that has the Devil popping up on December 7, 1941, Pearl Harbor Day, but there was no national emergency surrounding a report of its appearance in Mount Holly in 1948. In 1949, a "green male monster" supposedly was seen at Somerville, New Jersey; unfortunately (or fortunately!) that is the extent of our information. Maybe that sighting even goes in the Lizardman file. As to the "male" parts of the story, perhaps we are indeed lucky to not know. In 1952, something killed large numbers of chickens on Atlantic County farms. Since Atlantic County is in Devil territory, locals held the beast responsible.

On October 31, 1957, state newspapers asked in the headlines of front-page stories, "Is Jersey's 'Devil' Dead? Skeleton Baffles Experts." Said the stories, "The Jersey Devil may have met his final end this summer in the depths of the Wharton Tract down in the pine barrens of central South Jersey. Foresters and other members of the New Jersey Department of Conservation and Economic Development at work on the state-owned property report the finding of a partial skeleton, half-bird and half-beast, and impossible of conventional identifications." It was a Halloween gag, of course.

But five students from the Spring Garden Institute at Philadelphia were not amused when "unearthly screams" kept them awake one night in 1960 as they camped near Lake Atsion in Burlington County. "We were pretty much on edge," said Bert Schwed, one of the group, "after finding four large tracks earlier in the underbrush near our camp. They were about 11 inches long and they looked something like a large bird print with the heel dug in and the toes spread out."

Over in Dorothy, near Mays Landing, in October of the same year, residents complained to Game Warden Joseph Gallo that they were hearing weird cries in the night and discovering unusual tracks in the ground in the morning. After a brief investigation, Gallo and State Game Trapper Carlton Adams concluded that the tracks were caused by a large hopping rabbit whose feet touched the ground together to form one print, and that the noises were made by owls. Not terribly impressed by this official conclusion, locals said they knew an owl's screech when they heard it.

Shortly afterwards, the Broadway Improvement Association of Camden offered a $10,000 reward to anyone who could catch the Devil alive. "They do not seem worried about the prospect of having to pay up," the Trenton *Times* noted sardonically.

Toward dusk on May 21, 1966, a creature "at least seven feet tall" ambled through the Morristown National Historical Park and left in its wake four hysterical witnesses who had viewed it from a parked car.

They said the creature was "faceless," covered with long black hair, and had scaly skin. It had broad shoulders and walked on two legs with a stiff, rocking movement. (Is this a candidate for the Lizardman file too?)

The four drove to the park entrance and stopped approaching cars to warn people that a "monster" lurked inside. Raymond Todd, one of the witnesses, caught a ride with a young lady who took him to the Municipal Hall in Morristown, where he blurted out his story to the police. Oddly enough, the girl had seen a similar entity a year before. She told police that she and several friends were in the park one night when a huge, broad-shouldered something had loomed up in their rear window and thumped on the back of the car. Her mother had asked her not to report the incident, she said.

Or was it Bigfoot? Creatures reported with the characteristics of Bigfoot have been called the Jersey Devil for a long time.

Underneath all the myth, all the nonsense, all the fabrication, could here be a small core of truth from which the legends have grown? There are many loose ends—like tracks and sightings by reliable witnesses—that can no longer be glossed over. But it is difficult to move beyond these simple and by now fairly obvious conclusions. To start with, nothing precisely like a "Jersey Devil" has ever been reported elsewhere. But then the same is true of those entities called "Mothman," whose activities seem confined generally to certain southeastern states.

Mothman and the Jersey Devil share other traits as well. For one thing both supposedly possess wings; they also sometimes "glow" or "flicker" in the dark, although most of those descriptions may be pegged on reflections. The differences, however, are greater. Witnesses have reported three Mothman types: a winged quasi-humanoid, an enormous bird, and a mechanical contrivance. None of these bears much resemblance to the ram-headed, horselike, flying Jersey Devil. Moreover, Mothman glides through the air with the greatest of ease; the Devil on the other hand flies clumsily and close to ground level and can negotiate only short distances at a time. Of course, there is no shortage of winged weirdies of all sizes and varieties around the world, so we should not hold the Devil's distinctive shape against the poor fellow. But just what is that distinctive shape?

Assuming for the moment the Devil exists at all, one would figure the creature probably most resembles what was observed in January 1909. These reports are more detailed than most others and at the time the press treated them with reasonable objectivity.

But the 1909 reports are very suspect. Nearly two centuries after the creature's reputed birth, this rash of bizarre sightings erupted in the first decade of the twentieth century. The episode has been dubbed the Jersey Devil's "finest hour." In the course of five January days, more than one hundred persons across eastern Pennsylvania and southern New Jersey swore they had seen the beast. All over the region accounts of such a creature or creatures were heard, as well as the discoveries of bizarre, unidentifiable hoofprints in the snow. Schools and businesses closed. Newspaper articles were written and read.

A climax to the events took place on January 21, in West Collingswood, when the town's fire department supposedly confronted the monster and sprayed it with fire hoses as it swooped menacingly overhead. The next morning, a Camden woman said the Jersey Devil attacked her pet dog. This report marked the end of the 1909 flap, although another solo sighting occurred in February.

But years later, detailed information provided to author Loren Coleman in a long letter from early cryptozoologist Ivan T. Sanderson, a longtime New Jersey resident, spoke of some long-ignored discoveries he had made. Sanderson offered a likely explanation for the scare—apparently an elaborate real estate hoax. Sanderson even found in an old barn the fake feet used to make the footprints in the snow. Hoofprints and other evidence were faked or misidentified. The stories of sightings seem to have been a combination of planted stories, hoaxes, and imaginations fueled by fear.

Crafty trickster-purchasers wanted to buy up rural property that speculators had identified as soon-to-have increased values because of planned development. The thought was that the ill informed and those scared of the Jersey Devil activities would gladly sell their land to "fools" who wanted to take their "worthless" real estate off their hands.

Despite the hoaxes of the past, however, we must ponder that perhaps several Jersey Devils do haunt the Pine Barrens, including flying lions and kangaroos, or in any case creatures that looked like that to flustered individuals seeing them in less than ideal light conditions. Most of the folklore, though, clearly takes its inspiration from those alleged run-ins with a beastie of the 1909 variety.

Not everything that gets shoved under the Jersey Devil banner really belongs there. Like other states, New Jersey harbors more than one mystery animal, but whenever one appears, inevitably it gets hailed, usually for purposes of ridicule, as the latest manifestation of the Devil and so joins the great body of myth, legend, and lore.

The descriptions sometimes do go all over the map. The *Observer-Tribune* of October 27, 2005, carried an article about the "Great Swamp Devil." The Great Swamp is only twenty-six miles west of Times Square. The descriptions of the Great Swamp Devil, "stalking visitors to Great Swamp for 100 years," run the gamut "from a tall hairy man to a winged beast." It has even been reported to have "glowing liquid red eyes."

Are the Great Swamp Devil sightings merely one and the same as the Jersey Devil? There have been Bigfoot sightings from the Great Swamp as well. The article said, "a plan to build an airport by the Port Authority in the late 1950s was squashed by local activists and [the swamp] was named a national wildlife refuge. Bigfoot did not squash the refuge, though. One man said there was a sighting in the 1970's." Was this truthful reporting or a modern newspaper hoax?

When Sasquatch researcher John Green came to New Jersey in the 1970s, he was struck by how Bigfoot-type reports were being called Jersey Devil sightings. Pumas or phantom black panthers may deserve blame for at least some of the livestock kills. The last year of normal *Felis concolor* (mountain lion) abundance in New Jersey was 1840, but the behavior of the rampaging creature of that same year suggests that it could have been a phantom panther.

More modern sightings, if taken seriously, remind us that a diverse number of creatures have been lumped under the Jersey Devil rubric. In one recent sighting from December 1993, a witness named John Irwin, a summer park ranger in the Wharton State Forest of New Jersey and a respected figure in the community, was patrolling at night when he noticed a large, dark figure emerging from the woods. It stood like a human, more than six feet tall, and it had black fur, which looked wet and matted. The forest service report of the incident went on to state the following:

> John sat in his car only a few feet away from the monster. His initial shock soon turned to fear when the crea-

ture turned its deer-like head and stared through the windshield. But instead of gazing into the bright yellow glow of a deer's eyes, John found himself the subject of a deep glare from two piercing red eyes.

As a joke, some New Jersey researchers compared what Irwin saw to the Australian Bunyip, because the Bunyip is as ill-defined as the Jersey Devil. Of course, recent reports like John Irwin's fit easily into the Bigfoot file, too.

Meanwhile, the strangeness continues unabated. In late 1995, Sue Dupre was driving near Pompton Lakes when a hopping animal with an armadillo-like face raced across the highway. Clearly, more and more sightings have taken place. (For your reference, the appendix on page 97 gives a chronological, graphic, and comprehensive listing of Jersey Devil sightings and encounters.) What is perhaps even more significant in the last fifteen years is the enormous cultural impact that the Jersey Devil has had across the board in our society and within the new digital era of cable television and music.

As the last century ended, the morphing presentation of the Jersey Devil made, as earlier noted, a showing in the television series *The X-Files*. In an early episode, the Jersey Devil appeared as a feral, half-human female, a not-too-distant shadow of Bigfoot. On the Web site *TV Squad*, Anna Johns wrote of her interest in the episode "The Jersey Devil" in her blog:

> Season one of *The X-Files* is phenomenal. I had forgotten how many terrific episodes were packed into the first season. Chris Carter really seemed to have this show down solid right out of the gate. He set up the series with aliens, government cover-ups and monsters; and episode five of season one introduced us to the agents.

> We learn that [FBI Agent Fox] Mulder lives and breathes his work. He and [FBI Agent Dana] Scully travel up to Atlantic City, New Jersey, where Mulder butts heads with the local PD, who have jurisdiction over the case of a Bigfoot-looking creature that is killing homeless people. Mulder thinks it's the famous Jersey Devil, which chewed a man's arm off in the 1960s.

Johns mentioned the side trips taken by agents Mulder and Scully, but then comes back to the Jersey Devil. She concludes the following in her overview:

> Mulder ends up coming face-to-face with The Jersey Devil, a woman who was evidently raised in the forest just outside of Atlantic City. Scully just misses seeing the missing link when Mulder is attacked. But, for once, Mulder is vindicated when he and Scully catch up to the naked, hairy woman. Unfortunately, they don't get any answers from the woman because the trigger-happy sheriff's department kills her (and tastefully covers up her private parts with leaves).

The 1998 film *The Last Broadcast*, produced by Stefan Avalos and Lance Weiler, has a four-man group going into the Pine Barrens in search of the Jersey Devil. When three of the four do not emerge from the Barrens, and then the fourth individual dies by suicide, the mystery unfolds around the analysis of the surviving film footage found at the crime scene. Shot with a budget of only $900, the movie went on to gross $4,000,000, making it a very profitable independent film.

The century roared to a close and opened with more Jersey Devil appearances in popular culture. In 2002, an episode of *Scariest Places on Earth* dealing with the Jersey Devil aired.

On Halloween 2008, Bruce Springsteen released on his Web site a music video and free audio download single entitled, "A Night with the Jersey Devil." It opened with the following note: "Dear Friends and Fans, If you grew up in central or south Jersey, you grew up with the Jersey Devil. Here's a little musical Halloween treat. Have fun!" Coincidentally, the next day, Darren Deicide released his third CD, *The Jersey Devil is Here*, at a Day of the Dead CD release party at the Lamp Post Bar and Grille in Jersey City.

Also in 2008, the History Channel program *MonsterQuest* aired an episode set in and around the Pine Barrens presenting the history, current evidence, and eyewitness reports of the creature. Javier Ortega noted on the Web site *Ghost Theory* that "It was a well put together show that was focused on facts. An interesting tidbit of information was learning that Napoleon Bonaparte's brother, Joseph, had reported to have encountered the creature in the early 1800s during a hunt in the Pine Barrens."

The rest of the *MonsterQuest* episode centered on recent sightings of the mythical creature, and with thin speculative evidence, skeptically suggested that the creature may be a great horned owl or other known predatory bird.

The 2009 film *Carny* featured the Jersey Devil wreaking havoc on a small town in Nebraska after it was hauled there as an attraction in a traveling carnival. Also that year, the Jersey Devil appeared in the Animal Planet cryptozoology series *Lost Tapes*.

Lastly, and most recently, on February 2, 2010, on the season finale of the A&E reality television series *Paranormal State*, the film crew went to the Devil's traditional Jersey home, the Pine Barrens. They went to the Leeds farm and allegedly captured the Jersey Devil on infrared footage that was shown in the episode.

What was seen on screen during series episode 66 and the finale of Season 4 was a rather strange-looking, off-balance creature appearing to point up into the air at a 45-degree angle, with alleged wings and what appeared to be an oversized head on its body. Was it an owl or a duck? Or perhaps, as Javier Ortega at *Ghost Theory* wondered aloud, "that either this is just a tree branch that is reflecting the deer's body heat, some false wings put on a domesticated deer for the purpose of a hoax, or the Jersey Devil itself. Given that this is their season finale, my guess is that the producers wanted to go out with a bang!"

Reality-based television programming like *MonsterQuest*, *Lost Tapes*, and *Paranormal State* have certainly done one thing as we enter the twenty-first century. They collectively have kept the Jersey Devil mystery of the Pine Barrens quite alive and well. Viewers have been intrigued by the possibility that the creatures we call the Jersey Devil actually do exist.

Is there a Jersey Devil? We remain open-mindedly skeptical and hope that in the future someone will make a discovery or report a sighting that will settle the question once and for all.

Mystery cryptids of many kinds—little otter-shaped animals, hairy bipeds, strange birds, unknown panthers—that are seen in New Jersey are now always referred to as Jersey Devils, though surely none really are.

In the meantime we are convinced of this much: The Jersey Devil is more than just a legend, more than a centuries-old folktale, and more than a convenient gimmick for hucksters to use in fooling the unsuspecting. It is all these things, true, but it is also something else—a mystery.

More Winged Wonders and the Wooo-Wooo

If the Jersey Devil isn't enough to fear, there are other winged wonders in the skies of New Jersey to worry about, too. Perhaps the most forgotten and least frightening monster is a bird of fiction. As noted by an unknown author at the popular Web site *io9*, here is one you will not find in any of your history books:

> A giant chicken terrorizes Hoboken in Daniel Pinkwater's young-adult novel *The Hoboken Chicken Emergency* (1977). Later made into a movie, the novel is great stuff—goofy and smart—plus it's the only story we can think of about giant chickens set in New Jersey.

But back to reality, of sorts, in our quest for the feathered Fortean fowl of our state under study. New Jersey seems to have been the destination of a most grotesque assortment of man-birds seen headed in from New York, from September 1877 through 1880. They fit perfectly well in the context of other winged weirdies from around the country.

William H. Smith saw a winged human form moving over Brooklyn, New York, on September 18, 1877. In September 1880, a black man with bat's wings was seen flying over Coney

Island toward New Jersey. The figure had a peculiar expression about it. On September 12, 1880, the *New York Times* announced the following to its readers:

> One day last week, a marvelous apparition was seen near Coney Island. At the height of at least 1000 feet in the air a strange object was in the act of flying toward the New Jersey coast. It was apparently a man with bat's wings and improved frog's legs. The face of the man could be distinctly seen and it wore a cruel and determined expression. The movements made by the object closely resembled those of a frog in the act of swimming with his hind legs and flying with his front legs. . . . When we add that this monster waved his wings in answer to the whistle of a locomotive and was of a deep black color, the alarming nature of the apparition can be imagined. The object was seen by many reputable persons and they all agree that it was a man engaged in flying toward New Jersey.

Birdmen reports like the above started in earnest in America with the July 29, 1880, issue of the Louisville, Kentucky, *Courier-Journal*. The story reported that two local residents, C. A. Youngman and Ben Flexner, had seen what they at first took to be the wreck of a toy balloon in the sky the night before. But when the flying contraption came closer, the witnesses saw that it was really "a man surrounded by machinery which he seemed to be working with his hands." Wings or fins were protruding from his back, they reported, and the apparatus seemed to be propelled by their flapping. When the contraption began to descend, the flier would make the wings move faster and he would then ascend and continue flying along a horizontal path. Eventually he passed out of view and into the twilight.

Another flying creature apparently returned to the American skyways several years later. On April 16, 1897, a weird apparition sailed over Mount Vernon, Illinois. Was it a Jersey Devil clone? According to the Saginaw *Courier Herald*, more than a hundred people saw the gargoyle. "It was first observed about 8:30," reports the paper, "and continued in sight for half an hour. Mayor Wells, who had an excellent view of the mysterious visitor from the observatory attached to his residence, says it resembled the body of a huge man swimming through the air with an electric light on his back."

UFO investigator Gray Barker mentions in his *Book of Saucers* that he discovered an article in a 1922 edition of the Lincoln, Nebraska, *Daily Star*, quoting an eyewitness who had seen a large circular object land near his house from which an eight-foot-tall being emerged. This is significant, as author John Keel pointed out:

> Dr. Jacques Vallee found a remarkably similar report from Nebraska in that same year, 1922, in a letter buried in the Air Force UFO files at Dayton, Ohio. The letter writer, William C. Lamb, was hunting near Hubbell, Nebraska (yes, Nebraska, as in *Carny*), when, at 5:00 A.M. on Wednesday, February 22, 1922 he heard a high-pitched sound and saw a large, dark object pass overhead, blotting out the stars. He hid behind a tree, he said, and watched as the object landed. Next he saw "a magnificent flying creature" which landed like an airplane and left tracks in the snow. It was at least eight feet tall. It passed by the tree where Lamb was hiding, and he tried to follow its tracks but never managed to catch up with it.

How about the Giant Owl of New Jersey? The bald peaks of the Carolinas, the Appalachians of the East, the Ozarks of the

Midwest, and the Rockies out west have their various giant bird accounts, but have you heard about New Jersey's Wooo-wooo?

The Wooo-wooo, like the giant owl that became known as the Mothman of West Virginia, was given a very distinctive name. Mark A. Hall documents the encounters with this avian wonder in the privately published 1988 edition of his book *Thunderbirds!: The Living Legend of Giant Birds*. The passage is not found in the later version of the book, which was published by Paraview Press:

> The source for this story is a famous naturalist and author, Ivan T. Sanderson. . . . In June 1965 he had an unexplained experience of his very own on his farm in northwestern New Jersey. His farm was located in some low hills that rise out of a famous geological feature, the Great Valley. This valley extends from the Hudson River Valley southwesterly all the way to the state of Alabama. In northern New Jersey the boundaries of the Great Valley are the Kittatinny Ridge and Jenny Jump Mountain. From an overlook on the road to Great Meadows that winds up the northwest face of Jenny Jump there is a view to the northwest across the Valley to the Delaware Water Gap that cuts the Ridge. Halfway between the overlook and the Gap is the farm where early one morning Sanderson and two colleagues, Walter McGraw and Tom Allen, heard a strange sound. They had backed a loaded station wagon to the back door of the farmhouse to unload equipment. They were surrounded by sound of wildlife. The backyard was encompassed by trees. Nearby a sizable patch of woods was kept in a wild state. Also a small pond and an area of swamp had been purposely created by dams on a

creek that ran close to the farmhouse. According to Sanderson's account, the birds, the frogs, and all nearby wildlife suddenly became silent.

Only after the silence began did they hear a loud animal cry Sanderson described as "WOOoo-WOOoo-WOOoo." The sound grew louder—and seemingly closer—until the noise was almost painful to the ear. Then the sound receded as if the maker were moving away until it was heard no more. Sanderson was of the opinion that this sound was made by something moving rapidly down the Kittatinny Ridge. In addition to an echo, they thought they heard a second call from the area of Bangor, Pennsylvania, across the Delaware River. The two calls blended and went south. After five minutes the normal animal sounds resumed.

Sanderson later found one man who had encountered something making the same sound years earlier in the mountains west of Bangor. This man had also met three other people who had run into the "Wooo-Wooo," as Sanderson called it when he wrote of his experience in the Blairstown (New Jersey) *Press* for April 13, 1968. No one got a good look at this creature.

Hall also earlier had noted a case from the south in the same year with similar calls: "Merle Rose of Amarillo, Texas, did not have to leave home to see his giant bird in the summer of 1975. It perched on his house and made sounds like 'whoo, whoo, whoo.' When it took off its flapping wings 'sucked a whole bush from the ground' in front of him."

Last but not least, New Jersey appears in a story that reminds us of the hysteria in recent years caused by sightings of ivory-billed woodpeckers and the debates of their existence that are very active today.

Was the Garden State on the threshold of a similar wave of interest almost fifty years ago?

Sightings in 1965 at Homer, Michigan, and Park Ridge, New Jersey, were reported by Irene Llewellyn and Stella Fenell to be passenger pigeons (*Ectopistes migratorius*, the Latin name given by Carl von Linné in 1766), a species presumed extinct in 1914. Hope springs eternal, but the sighted birds were probably mourning doves (*Zenaida macroura*).

What the heck is going on in New Jersey? The strangeness has merely just begun.

Big Red Eye and Other Garden State Giants

Most people think of Bigfoot, if they consider it existing at all, as a phenomenon of the Pacific Northwest, a gigantic unknown primate that allegedly lurks in the rainy mountain forests of northern California, Oregon, Washington, and British Columbia. But what of New Jersey, the fifth smallest state and most densely populated? Could such a creature exist there, unseen by all but a lucky few?

The answer is . . . maybe. East Coast Bigfoot sightings actually go back to the days of the earliest colonists and beyond to folk tales of Native Americans. Algonquin legends told of the Wendigo, or Windigo, a hairy, giant, sometimes cannibalistic "man" who was greatly feared. Many Iroquois tales were told of encounters with Bigfoot-like creatures they called "Stone Giants."

In 1604, famed French explorer Samuel de Champlain, for whom Lake Champlain on the New York–Vermont border is named, sailed up the St. Lawrence River, where the local Micmac tribe told him stories of the Gougou, a giant, hairy, manlike beast. In 1759, during the French and Indian War, Maj. Robert Rogers and his band of rangers exploring northern Vermont reportedly encountered "a large black bear" that attacked them by throwing stones and other large objects. The local Indians called the creature "Wet Skine," or "Wet Skin," and claimed that it was not a bear but something quite different.

The best-known East Coast Bigfoot is probably Florida's Skunk Ape, which not only has its own Web site, but was the subject of a feature in the *London Times* on February 18, 2008. The article, entitled "The Skunk Ape: Florida's Answer to the Abominable Snowman," was written by Jacqui Goddard, and it detailed the background of the colorfully named creature, so-called because of its musky, unpleasant odor. Goddard wrote of a 2005 incident in which "a Florida cryptozoologist claimed to have been hit on the head by a skunk ape armed with a stick; and in 1975 another was seen tottering along a roadside with an armful of stolen corn."

Another article, called simply "The Skunk Ape of Florida," was published in *The Ledger* in Florida's Polk County on October 28, 2007. Written by Cinemaon Bair, it delved into the ancient origins of the beast: "The Seminoles call him Esti Capcaki, but most Floridians know him as the 'skunk ape.' And he's sparked imaginations and debate for nearly two centuries." The author went on to note that more than 350 Skunk Ape encounters have been reported throughout the state.

In the book *Florida's Unexpected Wildlife*, author Michael Newton claimed that "Florida's list of sightings rivals that of the Pacific Northwest, where Bigfoot/Sasquatch has beguiled explorers and researchers since the early 19th century." Newton went on to describe an incident in 1818, "when Apalachicola residents reported seeing a five-foot-tall 'baboon,' pursuing it to a makeshift nest amid cotton bales stored on the north side of town."

Perhaps because the beast favors semi-tropical swamps such as the Everglades, its putrid smell seems to be worse than that of your average, garden-variety Bigfoot. In *Weird Florida*, Charlie Carlson wrote, "It's this skunk-like stink that gives the skunk ape its name, although old-timers in rural areas often refer to it as 'swamp monkey.'"

One of the authors of this book, Loren Coleman, has noted in his writings that the Skunk Apes are much more anthropoid than the reports of the generally considered Eastern Bigfoot or modern Windigo, which appear to be decidedly hominid. But guess where a lot of people from New Jersey take their vacations? That's right, Florida; so the Skunk Ape reports might be in the minds of folks who may be seeing things near home in New Jersey.

Back up north in the Mid-Atlantic states, New York State has been surprisingly active for Bigfoot reports. One might not expect the state that is home to "the city that never sleeps" to be a hotbed of cryptozoological activity, but New York (outside the city, that is) has a long and rich history of such encounters. The *New York Herald* of November 29, 1893, for example, reported a case in Rockaway Beach on Long Island in which a large "wild man" frightened several local people.

The *Daily Press* of August 29, 1895, featured a report from Delaware County in which a "wild man" seized a traveler's horse, killed it, and dragged it away. Before the name "Bigfoot" became part of the language, all hairy, manlike bipedal creatures were referred to as "wild men."

There was a series of reports in 1909 (yes, that important Jersey Devil year), again on Long Island, of a "baboon" or "monkey-like" creature that was seen by residents of the towns of Patchogue, Quogue, Eastport, and Westhampton. Witnesses claimed the beast made "a blood-curdling shriek."

In early November 1922, armed police and civilian patrols searched the Long Island community of Babylon after sightings were reported of a "baboon" or "gorilla." In 1922, the

Washington Post reported on November 6 that a "four-foot baboon" was seen in the woods of Babylon. According to locals, it was "known to have lived in a vacant house for two weeks" and it attacked thirteen-year-old Willie Erlinger, who was unharmed but very shaken.

Long Island was a virtual hotbed of Bigfoot reports in the early thirties. The *New York Times* of June 30, 1931, featured an article about a mysterious four-foot anthropoid seen briefly by people in a nursery in Mineola. Armed police found no trace of the animal. In a possibly related incident, the Stockman family saw a "gorilla-like animal running through shrubbery" near Huntington, Long Island, on July 18, 1931, as noted by famed anomalistic researcher and author Charles Fort in his book *Wild Talents*. Later that July, again near Huntington, a farmer saw a "strange animal" and police found tracks, but nothing seemed to come of the investigation. And all through the early thirties, an eight-foot-tall "gorilla with glowing red eyes" was spotted on several occasions in the town of Amityville, later to be the location of a famous haunting.

Mundane and spectacular East Coast Bigfoot reports have come from upstate New York. In the summer of 2009, the History Channel series *MonsterQuest* produced an episode called "New York Bigfoot." It featured interviews with eyewitnesses to a 1976 sighting in the small town of Whitehall, nestled in the foothills of the Adirondack Mountains near Lake Champlain, the alleged home of "America's Loch Ness Monster," fondly known as "Champ." On August 25, 1976, Whitehall police officer Brian Gosselin, accompanied by a New York state trooper, saw a large, two-legged creature cross Abair Road, coming to within thirty feet of Gosselin's car. The seven- to eight-foot creature had, according to Gosselin, "big red eyes that bulged about half an inch off its face, no ears, no tail, dark brown hair, almost black; the arms swung down past its knees." After a minute or so, the trooper shone a flashlight into the beast's face and it ran off screaming.

There were also many reports of the so-called "Kinderhook Creature" in the Dutch colonial village of Kinderhook, New York, in the early eighties. On September 24, 1980, several of this book's coauthor's relatives, Martha Hallenbeck and her family, were terrorized on their McCagg Road property by a Bigfoot-like beast that made frightening vocalizations. A relative, Barry Knights, was called to the home and fired off several shots from his shotgun, whereupon the creature ran off shrieking. The late Dr. Gary Levine, a social sciences professor from Columbia-Greene Community College in Hudson, New York, investigated the sightings and noted that the swampy area known as Cushing's Hill, from which many locals felt the creature came, was very similar to the marshy woodlands in New Jersey where he had investigated other Bigfoot reports.

In fact, there may be a direct connection between sightings of Bigfoot creatures in New York and New Jersey. Late cryptozoologist Dr. Warren L. Cook, a professor of history and anthropology at Castleton State College in Vermont, opined that Bigfoot creatures might be migratory. He felt that many of the sightings between Vermont, New York, and New Jersey might have been of the same individual creatures.

Cook's research indicated to him that what is commonly referred to as Bigfoot is in fact a real flesh-and-blood biological animal, a highly intelligent being with a keen sense of smell and a strong knowledge of its territory. The screams it has been said to emit, Cook theorized, could be territorial calls similar to what apes and monkeys make in the wild.

These factors, combined with its apparently nocturnal nature, physical strength, and ability to keep itself hidden, may account for the sightings. Although no bones and only inconclusive biological evidence has been found to support the existence of the creatures, there are certain patterns that are consistent.

For example, the majority of sightings in upstate New York, such as those around Whitehall, take place in spring or summer. This makes perfect sense, of course, as more people are outdoors at that time of year and are therefore more likely to encounter something unusual. Many of the sightings that are reported in more southerly areas of New York, such as at Kinderhook, take place in the fall.

The Whitehall sightings involving the town and state police, to use one example, took place in August. The sightings in Kinderhook involving the Hallenbeck family took place in September and October. The reports in New Jersey follow a similar pattern, taking place in the fall and winter.

Could this mean that Bigfoot creatures migrate south as the weather turns colder? Cook felt that this was a distinct possibility. His theory was that these creatures lived in small breeding colonies of five to ten individuals. Barry Knights reported seeing "four great big furry things on two legs" in a swamp where he was trapping game in December 1979. He and his cousin, Russell Zbierski, reported hearing screams while walking near the Cushing's Hill area in November 1980 on a dark, cloudy night. Suddenly, "five hulking creatures with cone-shaped heads" converged in the road ahead of them. A third witness who lived just down the road reported a Bigfoot taking food out of her outdoor garbage can at roughly the same time.

Obviously, if Bigfoot creatures are biological animals, they must reproduce. But to avoid being seen by humans, which they seem to be very determined to do, they must also travel in very small groups through the most remote locations. Indeed, the most common Bigfoot reports on the East Coast tend to be of the creatures crossing roads, which they would have to do at some point. The human factor must be placed into the equation here, as roads are the natural point of overlap between mobile humans and Bigfoot on the move. The East Coast is far more heavily populated than the mountains of the Pacific Northwest, where Bigfoot reports tend to take place in more remote locations.

One of the earliest encounters with a Bigfoot in New Jersey was reported in the January 9, 1894, edition of the *New York Herald*. The headline read, "Wild man hunt in New Jersey." The article began as follows:

> There is a wild man in the woods near Mine Hill, and though parties that have been hunting for him for several days have often felt cold in their heavy coats, the object of the search seems to get away comfortably with no more protection from winter chill than an abundant set of whiskers.

The story went on to detail the experience of "three mill girls" who saw the creature, and upon doing so, "they shrieked so loud and long that the business of the mill and nearly the whole town came to a standstill."

The creature, in turn, "gave an answering shriek of terror and took to the woods."

Eventually, hounds that belonged to two brothers, woodcutters named Bill and Mike Dean, cornered the "wild man." Bill was quoted as saying, "It's a bear or some varmint," although it certainly couldn't have been a bear, as it was described as "a savage looking figure. . . . His face was thickly covered with a dark, unkempt beard." The "varmint" then "looked savagely at the wood choppers for an instant and then sprang to the rocks," where "he picked up a club and brandished it. One of the dogs sprang at him and received a blow that nearly killed it."

The brothers fled to the company store and used the telephone to call for help. A search party was organized and "fifty men scoured the mountains" without finding the "wild man," who had disappeared into the dense underbrush.

The Bigfoot Casebook by Janet and Colin Bord reported an incident that took place in New Jersey in 1927:

> A New Jersey taxi-driver had an alarming experience . . . on his way to Salem one night. In wooded country he had a flat tire and stopped to change the wheel. He had just finished when the car began to shake. Looking up he saw "something that stood upright like a man but without clothing and covered with hair." He drove off so fast that he left his flat tire and jack behind. In Salem he told his story and two men drove back to investigate. They found the tire and jack, but no Bigfoot.

In the Pine Barrens, home of the Jersey Devil, two men camping allegedly had a pair of sightings of a Bigfoot-type creature, one sighting from only a few yards away. An "overpowering foul odor" was noticed.

New Jersey has been the home to many more Bigfoot encounters over the years. In *Strange Creatures from Time and Space*, author John A. Keel mentions an incident, which we also mention in the Jersey Devil section, near Lake Atsion in Burlington County in 1960. Five students from the Spring Garden Institute at Philadelphia reportedly heard "unearthly screams" while camping. One of the students, Berle Schwed, reported, "We were pretty much on edge after finding four large tracks earlier in the underbrush near our camp. They were about eleven inches long and they looked something like a large bird print with the heel dug in and the toes spread out."

There was another report in May 1965 from a young lady who was accompanied by three friends to Morristown National

Historical Park. She said that they had been parked in a dark spot when they heard a thumping on the back of their car. They looked out the rear windshield and saw "a huge form standing over the car. It was very tall and had broad shoulders." They drove away "in a state of panic" but didn't report the episode to the authorities at the time, as the girl's mother had urged her "not to mention the incident to anyone."

Almost a year later, on April 15, 1966, the Trenton *Evening Times* carried a story asserting that a "wave of animal disappearances was taking place in Burlington County." Stanley Silcoch was quoted as saying he thought he had solved the mystery when he shot a raccoon on April 8, but his two dogs mysteriously disappeared shortly afterward. State Trooper Alfred Potter found a footprint "so large a man's hand could not cover it."

On May 21, 1966, Raymond Todd and three of his friends saw a seven-foot black Bigfoot walking through a park near Morristown. It's another of those frustrating stories that comes down to us with very few details, but the fact that there was a witness who was willing to give his name lends the story some credence.

Are such cases as the Spring Garden Institute case and the various Morristown reports of Bigfoot or of the Jersey Devil? In *The Bigfoot Casebook*, the authors wrote of the following fascinating case reported by Bob Jones of the unexplained mysteries investigation group Vestigia:

> It was in the autumn of 1966 near Lower Bank, New Jersey, when a couple first found 17-inch, five-toed tracks outside their house after seeing a face peering in through a window that was over seven feet high. They started to leave scraps of vegetation outside, which were eaten. The only delicacy Bigfoot rejected was a peanut butter and jelly sandwich. On the night they

> failed to leave the scraps they heard a loud banging outside. When the husband went outside he found a gray-haired Bigfoot throwing a dustbin (garbage can) against the house wall. He fired a shot into the air, but Bigfoot did not budge, so he then shot at it and the creature ran off and did not return.

In the September 1977 issue of *FATE* magazine, a feature article by unexplained phenomena investigator C. Louis Wiedemann entitled "New Jersey Researchers Report Mysteries Breaking Out All Over" noted that some of the Bigfoot tracks found in New Jersey had three toes rather than the usual five. There also seemed to be some connection between the Bigfoot creatures seen there and UFO reports, which gets into some very weird territory indeed.

The author wrote, "As an officer of Vestigia, a newly formed New Jersey-based Fortean organization, I found myself in the thick of the situation—and even had a weird experience or two of my own." Wiedemann went on to relate an incident at White Meadow Lake, where he heard a strange vocalization: "It began as a forlorn howl but rose to something between a howl and a roar. In less than a minute it died away but the hair continued to stand up on the back of my neck."

Residents of the area had reported seeing "huge hairy bipeds and finding 17-inch footprints." During the same period, locals had also observed "strange lights . . . zipping and flashing through the night sky." Portions of dismembered animals had also been found along the edges of the woods.

According to Wiedemann, between February 1975 and December 1976 more than sixty separate eyewitness sightings of Bigfoot-type creatures were reported in the New Jersey counties of Morris, Warren, Hunterdon, and Sussex. A typical sighting came from a thirteen-year-old boy on August 1, 1976.

The boy and a seven-year-old companion had been picking berries in the woods early that morning when they spotted an enormous, hairy "monster." The story continued: "As they stared in astonishment, the crouching animal reared up to its full eight-foot height behind the patch of raspberry bushes. Before the boys could react, the beast took several giant steps and vanished into heavy foliage."

The younger boy claimed to have glimpsed the creature's face. "Blood was coming out of its eyes," he claimed. Wiedemann observed, "Vestigia investigators speculate that this might be a reference to the 'glowing red eyes', which Bigfoot witnesses often describe."

All of which brings us to Big Red Eye, a type of Bigfoot that has been prowling around the Garden State since at least the late nineteenth century. Sightings reached a peak in the 1970s and have since leveled off, but the creature has by no means left the state, especially the Sussex County area.

New Jersey's best-kept secret is that, despite its small size and large population, it also contains many farms and densely forested swamplands. In south Jersey, the Pine Barrens alone cover well over one million acres. It is not inconceivable, therefore, that a species of unknown primate may indeed dwell in some of the state's more remote areas.

According to the Vineland *Times Journal* of July 1972, two teenagers saw an eight-foot-tall Bigfoot at about 2 A.M. near a sand wash outside of Vineland. A farmer and his wife reported the same creature the next morning.

Unexplained phenomena investigator Robert C. Warth, attempting to explain a possible connection between ABSMs (Abominable Snowmen) and UFOs, interviewed a sixteen-year-old New Jersey girl on October 23, 1973, about her encounter with some creatures during a highly publicized wave of UFO reports. She told Warth that she saw a "Bigfoot with two young" standing on her front lawn in the middle of the night.

Cryptozoological connections with UFOs, while rare and an apparent artifact of the weird times of the 1970s, are hard to explain. These connections, nevertheless, are more common among East Coast Bigfoot reports than they are with the West Coast variety and suggest that some New Jersey Bigfoot creature sightings may have a kind of anomalistic "high strangeness" factor.

In February 1975, a motorist driving near the town of Bear Swamp reported that he twice saw a Bigfoot cross the road. There were other sightings at around the same time, again involving the creature crossing a road. Robert E. Jones, in an article titled, "Bigfoot in New Jersey?" wrote about these in Ivan T. Sanderson's SITU organization's journal, *Pursuit*.

In 1975, a forest ranger walking along a Sussex County trail saw a creature "about eight feet tall with big red eyes." Hence the creature's nickname, "Big Red Eye." High Point State Park is a hotbed of sightings, especially for park rangers, who generally don't want their names used in reports for fear of ridicule (or fear of losing their jobs).

In the summer of that same year, two boys riding their bicycles at dusk had an encounter with Bigfoot that shook them up pretty badly. As they were riding near a lake just outside of Rutherford, they saw a "Bigfoot nearly nine feet tall" on the trail ahead of them. Needless to say, they turned and took flight in the opposite direction.

Thirteen-year-old Lisa Farrell and two friends caught a glimpse of Bigfoot while playing in the woods near Ferrante's Quarry in Bernardsville in the summer of 1976. According to the Bridgewater *Courier News*, the girls also found three-toed footprints.

That same summer, *FATE* magazine featured an article by C. Louis Wiedemann, in which a woman reported that she saw a "large dark form" in her backyard at dusk. Later, she found five-toed, seventeen-inch footprints. The same article featured a report from a quarry worker who said that he saw a Bigfoot near the quarry in the daytime near White Meadow Lake. According to the witness, it seemed to have hair "longer than shoulder length."

On May 17, 1977, a headline in the *New Jersey Herald* screamed, "Wantage family in terror of odd creature for week." The article, written by Dave Shelton, began, "The police say it probably was a hungry bear that terrorized a family last week on Wolfpit Road, but members of that family who were less than 25 feet away from it say, 'It was something else.'"

The story went on to note that Barbara Sites, the mother of six children, said that the creature they had seen "was seven feet tall, covered with hair, had a beard and mustache and walked on its hind feet." She related that she had gone out that Tuesday morning to let her dairy herd into the pasture and that the cows had seemed "reluctant." At the same time, she heard a sound in the distance that she described as "like a woman screaming when she was being killed." She found her heavy wooden garage door torn from its hinges, and in the barn, she found six of the family's pet rabbits dead or mutilated. Two of them were missing and the head or legs were ripped off from the bodies of the others.

None of the rabbits had been eaten, but there was very little blood around the bodies, as though whatever had killed them had drained them dry. Sites told Shelton, "There were hardly any marks on two of them. . . . They just looked like someone squeezed them to death." Sites said that she ran from the barn and, with "several relatives and friends," saw "a big shadow—his head was high as the eaves."

The next night, the Sites family waited for whatever it was to return, with several relatives stationed in the farmyard armed with shotguns and rifles. At approximately the same time as the previous night, it showed up, appearing under the mercury-vapor lamp that lit up the yard. Sites recounted, "At first all I saw were these two red eyes staring at me from over there." Sites and the others fired upon the thing, using up more than thirty rounds of ammunition from a .410 shotgun, a 12-gauge shotgun and two .22-caliber rifles. The creature ran into the chicken coop and then came out from a window at the other end. Sites said, "He had his hands up in the air and I fired again. I thought he was coming at me." The creature didn't attack him, however. Instead, it escaped through the apple orchard and into the woods.

A follow-up story appeared in the *Herald* on May 20. The headline this time read, "Authorities call Wantage beast 'an unidentified woods animal.'" The state police and the New Jersey Division of Fish and Game had changed their story. Now they felt it may have been a wild dog, rather than a bear, that killed the rabbits and caused the commotion on the Sites farm. State police sergeant Ernest Seremi was quoted as saying that patrols had been checking the area around the farm for a week, but had been unable to identify any animal "capable of the attack." The new theory, according to Seremi, was "that the perpetrator is some type of woods animal, possibly a raccoon or wild dog, with little likelihood of it being a bear."

Obviously, the state police were just ignoring the eyewitness reports of a huge bipedal creature with "two red eyes" and "hands," as the Sites family had reported. They had their own theories and didn't want to be confused with the facts, as it were. Meanwhile, the article reported, "Two groups of volunteers, the Society for the Investigation of the Unexplained [Ivan Sanderson's group] and Vestigia, are probing the Sites farm for evidence of 'Bigfoot,' an alleged man-like creature said to have been spotted in that county, but never proven to exist."

Unfortunately, as is so often the case with Bigfoot reports, there were no further follow-ups, at least as far as the local media were concerned. Perhaps the Sites family was fed up with what they perceived as the unbelieving attitude of the police and the Division of Fish and Game.

The following year, however, two eleven-year-old boys reported seeing what they believed to be a Bigfoot near the town of Hopatcong, also in Sussex County. In 2001, on the Bigfoot Field Research Organization Web site, "Witness E.V." recalled of the incident, "He was about eight or nine feet tall and was walking horizontal to us. It was walking from right to left and was walking towards a small stream. It didn't seem to care about us, but we didn't stick around to find out."

In 1981, in the Newark Watershed of New Jersey, two fishermen saw a creature covered with reddish-brown hair when it strode across the road in front of their car. They followed it down a path and got to within five feet of it before their car got stuck in the mud. They got a good look at it, and said it was about 6.5 feet tall and had a flat face and human ears. It walked with a slight hunch, swinging its arms like a cross-country skier. One of the men said, "I'll go to my grave knowing it wasn't a bear or anyone in a suit. I don't expect to ever see anything like that again." Police said that bears were being seen in the watershed area, but the description given by the men who saw it from five feet away does not in any way resemble a bear.

"Bigfoot terrorizes Sussex" was the lurid headline almost two decades later, on November 1, 1998, in a Sussex County publication called *The College Hill*. Here is the beginning of the feature, written by Vashni De Schepper:

> Strange screams pierced the night and dogs were sent into a barking frenzy as an unseen creature prowled the

> outskirts of Sussex Borough. These nightly screams occurred over a two-week period this summer. The creature was usually heard between the hours of two A.M. and four A.M. By morning, the only evidence of its visits was some overturned garbage cans and a few frightened residents.

One anonymous ear-witness was quoted as describing the vocalization as "unlike any other sound I've ever heard before. It was like a mix between a bear and a cow." Another borough resident told De Schepper, "When the noises began, my cats started growling out the window. It was very frightening; they've never exhibited behavior like this before. Even the neighbors' dogs were barking like crazy."

The article went on to state that one J. D. Grant and another person had been walking on Layton Road in Sussex in 1996 when they encountered "a tall shaggy creature with red eyes," which stood near the edge of the road and watched them from approximately ten feet away. Grant was quoted as saying, "I knew it wasn't a bear, it was too lean and upright, it was humanoid."

De Schepper went on to state, "There are at least four other accounts, by independent witnesses, of a tall, shaggy creature with red eyes on this road." Another account occurred near Hainesville, in which two men supposedly came across a pair of dogs attacking a Bigfoot-like creature that was partially submerged in a beaver dam. The article continued:

> The men managed to drive the dogs away, and the creature that emerged from the swamp was about six feet tall and covered in hair. The majority of New Jersey Bigfoot sightings occur at night, near swamps, fields or crossing roads. The large stretches of wooded areas in Sussex County make it a perfect habitat for Bigfoot.

In the book *Weird N.J.*, by Mark Sceurman and Mark Moran, a witness known only as "Mike V." recounts his experience with Big Red Eye:

> One night, early last summer, we were walking our dog in our condo development (Paddington Square in Mahwah) and heard this guttural sound. It wasn't a dog or bear, but it was big and angry and had red eyes. It was roughly thirty yards from us. I told my wife to pick up the dog and go into the street and walk back home slowly. I was shaking in my boots as I slowly backed up, keeping my eyes on the brush. We made it home and called the police, not once, but twice, to find out what the hell that thing was. They investigated but found nothing.

The New Jersey Bigfoot Reporting Center is a sort of clearinghouse for the state's Bigfoot reports. A typically intriguing one is Report #97 from a witness who prefers to remain anonymous. It details a sighting that occurred on October 8, 1995, near Bassetts Bridge Road in Sussex. The witness had been fishing along the Wallkill River between 8:30 and 9:00 in the evening when he decided to go home because nothing was biting. When he turned to go to his car he saw something extraordinary standing about twenty-five feet beyond it. He described the creature:

> [It was] about eight feet tall. It had long thick hair covering its body, long arms (almost too long for its body), massive shoulders, no neck to speak of, and red glowing eyes. It did not seem threatening at all but I knew that if it wanted it could have had me for dinner.
>
> It made a low growling sound and turned its head slightly and I saw its eyes flicker like lit matches. I moved slowly to my car and left.

Drew Vics, owner of the New Jersey Bigfoot Reporting Center, offers his own theory as to the nature of the "glowing red eyes" on his Web site:

> Moonlight could have accounted for the apparent glowing effect of the eyes. Eyeshine would be the likely explanation, though it is not clear how the witness could have noticed any match-like flickering of the eyes at a distance of approximately 25 feet as estimated by the witness.
>
> Also to note, while red eyeshine is noticed in some animals native to New Jersey (foxes, rabbits, some owls, as well as bears and deer) . . . great apes are diurnal creatures, as are humans and so do not require a tapidum lucidum, the feature found on the retina of nocturnal animals which causes eyeshine and enhances vision in the dark.

Vics then goes on to opine on what he admits is "complete speculation" regarding Big Red Eye's most famous features:

> That great apes do not exhibit eyeshine is not to say that Bigfoot couldn't have adapted differently. Their elusiveness is often attributed to mainly nocturnal activity, so if these creatures exist and are a form of primate it is possible that they have evolved a tapetum lucidum to allow them enhanced nighttime vision.

Indeed, Bigfoot creatures from around the country and around the globe are often reportedly said to have red, self-illuminating eyes. On an October night in 1983, for example, three young men who were cycling near Lake George, New York, reported they had an encounter with something that made terrifying screams and that they then saw "big red eyes seven feet off the ground in the woods."

Under the heading of "Big Red Eye Takes a Holiday," Vics wrote on his Web site that witnesses in England had also reported sightings of "a giant, hairy creature with blazing red eyes." In the same article, Vics recounted that two New Jersey sightings had been reported to him recently. One was from a bow hunter in late 2004 who noticed a musky odor in the air, then saw a creature enter the forest trail. The witness described the creature as "broad-shouldered with no neck. The face appeared 'shiny' with less hair." The creature turned and looked in the hunter's direction, and then walked back into the wilderness near the Wanaque Reservoir.

Another sighting passed on to Vics occurred in 2005 in Riverdale, again near the Wanaque Reservoir. Some friends were sitting on a backyard deck talking, when one noticed "a grey-colored ape-like creature sitting some distance up a slope in the woods." One of the group went inside to retrieve a pellet gun. The popping sound of the gun "alerted the creature and it rose up, scaled a large boulder and stepped into the underbrush, out of sight."

The ubiquitous Big Red Eye, however, is not the only Bigfoot-type creature sighted in New Jersey. In October 1971, two teenagers were hiking through some dense woods in Essex County near Fairfield along a stream that fed into the Passaic River. Around noon, they observed four creatures from a distance of around seventy-five yards. The largest one was described on Vics' Web site:

> About eight feet tall, very long arms that went almost to the knees. Very powerfully built, barrel chested, very wide shoulders, the head seemed to have a rounded "peak." The color of all four was black; the faces

> seemed somewhat lighter in color, but not white. The second one was sitting on the ground, the third was lying on the stream bank and the last was standing in the middle of the stream.

If sightings of unknown primates are rare, then sightings of several of them together are almost unheard of. The teenagers recalled that they observed them for a few minutes, "and they also observed us." Then the youths took off and ran for home. Indeed, who could blame them?

Burlington County, which encompasses some of the Pine Barrens region, also has its share of reports. Some of the reports submitted to the Bigfoot Field Research Organization Web site include an October 1980 incident, in which bow hunters heard loud, high-pitched screams fifteen miles west of the Batsto River, near the Pine Barrens. High-pitched screams heard by hikers in the Pine Barrens were also reported in July 1991 as well as April 1997. There was a night sighting by motorists near the Garden State Parkway in July 1998. Driving near a wooded area, the anonymous witness recounted this:

> Here stood this man-like creature approximately seven feet tall, covered with hair from head to foot. Its head was hairy also, except for the areas surrounding the eyes, cheeks, and mouth. It appeared grayish in color from the headlights.
>
> In a split second, it turned and looked right at us. At the same time, it lifted its leg over the guardrail and disappeared down into the darkness of the woods.

A similar late-night sighting occurred in the fall of 2003 on Hogback Road near Bordentown. The witness recalled, "As we came around a bend in the road we noticed what seemed to be a primate-looking creature running across the road. It was upright but crouched over, using its arms to propel itself across the road." The witness continued, "This was no oversized monkey . . . it looked to be a dark brown color and the body covered in a thick shaggy-looking coat. It was roughly five feet in height hunched over. Its startling feature was its broadness." The creature vanished into the darkness of the woods.

Back up in north Jersey, Somerset County has its share of Bigfoot reports as well. The locals call it the Big Hairy Man, and it's been sighted from the Great Swamp area and the Somerset Hills, all the way to Hillside. Witnesses report that the creature stands about eight feet tall, walks upright, and is covered with reddish-brown hair. According to *Weird N.J.*, a bone specialist and a physical therapist encountered the beast while taking a shortcut through the Great Swamp on Lord Stirling Road. They claimed that the Big Hairy Man walked in front of their car and jumped the fence into the woods across the road. According to the Folklore Project in Bernardsville, sightings of the Big Hairy Man have been reported for many years.

Two witnesses who call themselves "MS" and "RS" recalled a 1976 sighting in *Weird N.J.* The report read, in part, as follows:

> If I had to guess it was a half man, half ape we spotted in the Bernardsville section of New Jersey. We've only told a handful of people about our encounter. Some feel we must have seen a bear, but we've never seen a bear swing his arms like a monkey or take strides like this thing did.

The *Courier News* in Bridgewater featured an article by Lore Fiedler in their February 19, 1979, issue with the heading, "'Bigfoot' Has Visited Bernardsville." He noted in his report that "Central Jersey believers had one to call their own two and a half years ago—the Bernardsville Bigfoot."

Three children in that Somerset Hills town claimed that they came across huge three-toed footprints, heard a creature go "thump" in the woods, and caught a glimpse of the beast while they were playing near Ferrante's quarry off Route 202. The incident occurred in the summer of 1976, "shortly after the hairy and scary giants were reported seen in Chatham and Rockaway Township in Morris County." According to the article, "The creatures were said to be nine feet tall and supposedly left 18-inch footprints, always with only three toes."

New Jersey resident and Web site designer John Carlson lives in the northeastern part of the state and presides over a blog called *Bigfoot in New Jersey*. Carlson's own wife, Debbie, a special education teacher, had an experience of the beastly kind, as he relates on his blog:

> Each June she accompanies her seventh grade class for a three-day outing at Stokes State Forest, which is in Sussex County and pretty close to Lake Owassa. Well, one night one of the students staying in the same cabin as Debbie had a severe asthma attack. The girl's parents didn't bother to notify the school about her condition and neglected to pack her inhaler, so my wife ran her out of the cabin at about three A.M. and proceeded to cross the compound to the infirmary where the nurse slept. As she ran toward the nurse's station she heard an awful yowling/screeching noise. It was very high-pitched and very loud, and unlike anything she'd ever heard before. It frightened her greatly. She did what she had to do, however, and alerted the nurse about the young girl's condition and an ambulance was called (the girl recovered, fortunately).

Carlson went on to relate that "the horrible screeching and yowling continued for several minutes" after his wife arrived at the nurse's station. A police officer arrived alongside the ambulance and Debbie asked the officer if he'd heard the sounds or if anyone else had reported them. Carlson wrote: "He looked at her and said in a very serious tone, 'There have been a lot of Bigfoot reports in the last few nights.'"

One of the respondents to Carlson's blog was a forty-six-year-old gentleman by the name of Robert J. Schneider, who grew up in Essex County. On February 10, 2010, he wrote this:

> My uncle owned a home in Layton, Sussex County, and my dad and I spent many days up there hunting, fishing and hiking. . . . I spent one weekend in the winter of '79 all alone at the house because a severe snowstorm trapped my dad and his brother in the city of Irvington. . . . Sometime after midnight I began to hear a screaming noise off in the woods behind the house, distant at first, so I thought the howling wind was playing tricks on me. The screams came at intervals every few minutes and were getting closer. I was so rattled by this, I went to the garage and let Molly, my uncle's German shepherd, in the main house and she was NEVER allowed in the house; my uncle would have kicked my butt if he had ever found out. The dog was spooked by the noises too; we spent the next couple hours huddled together near the fire until the screaming finally faded away. . . . That dog was as scared as I was, never saw her like that, never. These sounds were wild guttural screams and like nothing I'd ever heard before or since.

Well-known West Coast psychic Nancy Bradley had her own encounter with Bigfoot at Lake Owassa when she was a child. Her blog, posted on June 18, 2009, is quite evocative. She tells of Big John Lonewolf, a Ute Indian who was one of the few residents who lived on the lake all year round. Lonewolf, a proficient hunter and fisherman, told her tales of a huge "bearlike creature" that he was unable to catch. Her encounter with the creature occurred when she was about eight years old and was spending the summer at the lakefront cabin that belonged to her grandparents.

> An early evening . . . I chose to walk the two-mile small winding dirt road from our cabin to the "Boathouse" for an ice cream treat. . . . As I turned the final bend on the path, lights from the Boathouse were clearly in sight. Lagging along, I glanced into the woods beside me. There were two eyes fixated at me through the darkness.
>
> At first I thought it was a black bear . . . but this was a much larger creature, standing upright . . . about nine feet tall, and hiding behind a large oak. My view of the creature was obstructed because of all the brush, branches, and leaves. I began to walk faster as I strained to see further in its direction. Nothing moved except its eyes, which watched me pass.

Bradley finally reached her destination, the ice cream counter at the Boathouse, where she told the man who worked the counter what she had seen. She continued:

> He sat me down and handed me a glass of water. . . . To this day, I remember he had a strange look in his eyes, and he later had his son accompany me half-way back to our cabin, rifle in hand. . . . The next day he visited our cabin and told my grandmother he had encountered such a creature himself.

Paul Bartholomew is a veteran Bigfoot researcher from Whitehall, New York, near the Vermont border. He holds a bachelor's degree in journalism from Castleton State College, where he studied under anthropologist and Pulitzer Prize nominee Dr. Warren L. Cook. Bartholomew worked with Cook investigating area Bigfoot sightings for several years until Cook's death in 1989, when he was willed all of Cook's Bigfoot materials in the hopes that his work would live on. It did.

A research consultant for the 2004 Outdoor Life documentary *The Creature of Whitehall* and the 2006 History Channel documentary *Giganto: The Real King Kong*, Bartholomew is undoubtedly the go-to-expert for Mid-Atlantic Bigfoot sightings. In 2005, he made national headlines by successfully lobbying the Whitehall village and town boards to pass an ordinance making it an offense to harm any Bigfoot creatures within the township. In 2009, he co-authored with his brother Robert the book *Bigfoot Encounters in New York and New England*.

Interviewed for this book, Bartholomew offered his own insights as to what sort of unknown East Coast primates eyewitnesses are seeing. He feels that there's a lot of credence to the migration theory. "Dr. Cook believed that there was very good evidence there was a migration," Bartholomew said. "He felt that there was a certain migration route and they would maintain that route. He felt that there may have been a connection between the sightings in the Northeast and those further south."

Bartholomew and Cook both noticed a seasonal pattern in Bigfoot reports. "He (Cook) looked at regions during certain times of year," Bartholomew continued, "and found that the reports tended to cluster in Whitehall during summer, Kinderhook (farther south) in the fall, and New Jersey (still farther south) in the fall and winter. There was a Japanese researcher named Wasushi Kojo who came here to look up the locations of the sightings based on the *Monsters of the Northwoods* book, and he correlated a lot of the sightings that were left anonymous. He felt that we were dealing with a circular migration of several hundred miles."

The theory goes on to postulate that the creatures would travel in very small groups. According to Bartholomew, "Cook felt that the breeding pools would be small. That's why he felt that legislation and protective measures should be taken, because he felt that the death of even one could offset an entire community. He believed that these creatures were quite rare, which might also explain some of the nighttime vocalizations that are very loud and piercing; that they're actually communicating over large distances."

As for those big red eyes, "it's a very frequent characteristic," said Bartholomew. "The Abair Road incident in Whitehall, which turned out to be a landmark case for the Northeast because of all the police involvement, featured the red eyes as one of the distinguishing characteristics. In fact, in the original newspaper report in the *Glens Falls Post-Star*, the 'red glowing eyes' were noted."

Cliff Sparks had an encounter with something with "red glowing eyes" at his Skene Valley Country Club in Whitehall back in May 1975. Interviewed by host Mike Carnevale on the cable television show *Adirondack Journey* in 2008, Sparks recalled the incident:

> It was about eleven o'clock. It was an overcast night . . . this big thing, over seven feet tall, built like a monster, with terrific shoulders and long arms, was right in the middle of the green and he stared more at the dog than he did at me. . . . And there were these red lines coming out of its eyes, almost like laser beams, and the dog just hung its head over the cart and stayed there.

> And then this thing turned and ran up the crest into the woods. . . . It was almost like he (the dog) was paralyzed. It was so unusual for him. . . . It was like short lines that were going towards the dog—short red lines—it was weird.

Red glowing eyes sound almost occult. How can eyes glow from within? Bartholomew doesn't find the idea all that far-fetched. "This creature would most likely be categorized as being nocturnal, as it seems to travel a lot at night. Most of the sightings happen when motorists are driving along and the creature runs across the road in front of them. It may be that such a creature, nocturnal in nature, may have a different type of vision that we simply don't understand yet," he said. "Witnesses say over and over again that the eyes are not reflective; in other words, it isn't like the light shining off a cat's eye. It appears to be different. It appears to be a self-illuminating light. One of the old historical accounts refers to 'eyes glowing like embers.'"

Bartholomew feels there are connections not only between the sightings on the East Coast, but sightings around the world. "When investigator Paul Cropper was here from Australia, the Yowie (Australian Bigfoot) reports that he had looked into were almost interchangeable with what people were encountering here in the northeast," he recalled. "It appears to be a very similar type creature, but obviously there are regional characteristics. For example, the Skunk Ape in Florida seems to be more monkey-like and smaller in stature, while the Honey Island Swamp Monster in Louisiana is a little more aggressive. Some of the creatures are three-toed, some are five-toed, a very strange characteristic."

Bartholomew felt that it "would make perfect sense" if some of the creatures seen in New York and New Jersey were in fact the same individuals, migrating at various times of the year. "Being a constant mover," Bartholomew continued, "which is one of the migration theories, it could explain why the creature is sighted at, say, Abair Road in Whitehall in August of 1976 and again in August of 1979. It would explain why the West Rutland, Vermont, case in 1985 and Susan Cook's sighting in 1986 were exactly a year and a week apart. It keeps moving, but it's in certain areas at certain times."

And what is Bartholomew's current theory as to what these creatures might be? "I think if you look at the limited number of scientists who actually investigate this," Bartholomew said, "I guess the consensus would be that it's a form of Gigantopithecus [a large prehistoric anthropoid]. Among those who study it, that seems to be the prevailing theory. Some researchers simply believe that it's some form of unknown ape. I guess I would be leaning towards Gigantopithecus at this point," said Bartholomew.

Sightings of Big Red Eye and other New Jersey Bigfoot creatures continue to this day, and the Internet is proving to be a treasure trove of eyewitness reports. In the twenty-first century, mass communication is faster and more all encompassing than ever before, and it may be through blogs, videos, and Web sites that these unknown primates are finally identified by science once and for all. Of course, it will be a live capture or a dead body that ultimately solves the mystery.

Hoboken Monkey-Man and Urban Unknowns

It seems strange enough to find creatures such as Bigfoot and the Jersey Devil wandering about in the woods, but what do we make of reports of other odd cryptids seen in suburbia and even in the hearts of cities? "Curiouser and curiouser!" cried Alice, as channeled by Lewis Carroll, in *Alice's Adventures in Wonderland*.

Take, for example, the case of the so-called Hoboken Monkey-Man. In October 1982, rumors circulated throughout the entire Hoboken school system that there was a bizarre ape-like creature terrorizing students. It came to be known as the Hoboken Monkey-Man, as it was alleged to have been half-man and half-monkey.

Supposedly, the weird cryptid lurked in school hallways, attacked children on the way home from school, and threw students out of windows. It was even accused of killing a teacher.

Hysteria spread through the schools over a period of two weeks, so much so that the Hoboken police department set up a task force to investigate what was behind the rumors. Their job was to inform the students as to what was real and what was unreal about the alleged Monkey-Man. The Public Safety Council was also called in to help quell the students' fears.

But their inquiries came to a dead end. They could not find one student who had actually seen the Monkey-Man, nor was there any teacher who had been killed. Everything had happened to "a friend of a friend." No one the police spoke to had actually been attacked or "terrorized" by the mysterious beast.

In desperation, an official from the Public Safety Council finally pronounced, "There is no Monkey-Man, no students or children missing. We went looking for him, he wasn't even in the streets. How do you stop a rumor that's growing like wildfire?" The rumors did eventually die down, shortly after Halloween had come and gone.

This is not to say that all urban cryptid reports are merely rumors. There have been far too many sightings over the years of big cats, big birds, and even mystery kangaroos in urban areas to dismiss all of them as out of hand. The usual reason given for the presence of such out-of-place animals in such largely populated centers is that they "escaped from a zoo." Upon checking into local zoos, however, it is usually discovered that all of their animals are present and accounted for. And so the mystery deepens.

Strangely enough, there are other Monkey-Men that have been reported in New Jersey. On the *Weird NJ* Web site, a woman identified only as "Mary A." wrote this:

> About six years ago my children and I moved to Ninth Street in Bayonne, a dead end block. The end of the block drops off into Newark Bay. According to the kids in the neighborhood (and the parents too), no one is allowed to go down the hill to the bay and a fence has been erected to stop trespassers. After several weeks my children came home with a story explaining why no one is allowed down by the bay. Apparently there is an old PT boat factory at the bottom of the drop-off. A man lives there who is called "Monkey-Man."

According to my kids he was abandoned by his parents and has made his home there since he was a child. It is said he can be found wandering the trails along the Newark Bay. This past summer my kids say they saw him. According to them, he was wearing a ragged green shirt and had long brown hair on his arms. My younger son saw him again on the abandoned road walking with a dog. He said that he was wearing that same ragged green shirt. The road is gated and locked with chains and padlocks. How did he get in there? Very creepy.

An even stranger incident occurred to a woman named "Evelyn," as reported in the book *Weird N.J.* She had a strange encounter in Jersey City when she was ten years old:

> It was very quiet in the apartment, and I was reading. For some reason, I started getting a little spooked. I looked out the window at an apartment across the way, and I saw this man in a janitor's uniform, sweeping. But the weird thing was that he had a monkey's face with a human body! I yelled and woke up my father, but when we checked to see if he was still there, he was gone.

Following in the wake of the New Jersey Monkey Man flap of twenty years before, on the world scene, on May 1, 2001, the Indian media first published stories of their own Monkey Man Alert, about the sightings of hairy, four- to five-foot-tall ape-like creatures. For a two-week period, the so-called Monkey Man panic swept throughout India, mostly centered in the township of Ghaziabad, twenty-two miles north of New Delhi. The attacks of this giant monkey led to a major media event, which swept from India through the entire English-speaking world. More than one hundred different articles about the phenomena were published during the peak of the activity. More than a dozen people were hospitalized with fractures and severe injuries as a result of the attacks that occurred since April 28, many of them from falls suffered while running away.

In early April 2001, the creature was confined to Vijay Nagar when it started biting sleeping persons. It was then rumored to be a giant rogue monkey. These first witnesses said that a very tall monkey-like creature without a tail attacked them. The height of this creature was around five feet and it was hairy with large claws. People said that this creature attacked them without any provocation at all. The creature scratched the hands and necks of people mostly asleep late at night.

One witness, Ganesh Jha, of the Maharana Vihar Residents' Association, claimed he came face-to-face with the "huge man-monkey" and saw him jump 20 feet (6 meters) in the air. "We were taking an evening walk when we walked into this huge man-monkey. The monster sprang up 20 feet from a crouching position and grabbed the branches of a tree and vanished before me and my children could even scream," Jha told reporters.

From this small village the creature seems to have traveled to neighboring areas of the town of Ghaziabad. As more people grew aware of the sightings, hoaxes and exaggerations occurred. The original very tall monkey-like creature became a half-human with elephant-like legs, reddish hands, and metallic claws. Later, victims said it was a man with a monkey face, which soon became a masked man. Although the Ghaziabad police claimed that there was nothing like a Monkey Man, complaints of sightings, scuffles, and looting by the Monkey Man poured into police stations. At least two people died from falls from buildings (scared while sleeping on roofs) and more than fifty people were injured.

Finally, on May 16, 2001, the police in New Delhi, showing two different versions of the Monkey Man, issued a computer-generated sketch. Police said at the time they were no closer to solving the mystery of the ape-like creature and then finally quashed all further reports, saying it was mass hysteria. While the Monkey Man Alert resulted in panics more related to human psychology, some cryptozoologists feel that the initial sightings of the case, the first reported encounters with a large primate, may have had a zoological basis. The similar nature of the Indian accounts to the urban Hoboken reports of New Jersey's Monkey-Man is bizarre, to say the least.

Two park rangers reported a slightly less urban Monkey-Man a few years ago near the Atlantic County Park in New Jersey on Route 50. They both saw what they described as "an anthropoid, ape-like creature" crossing the road. At first glance, this sounds like a Bigfoot report, but it was described as a smaller sort of Monkey-Man. Neither ranger reported the sighting at the time, as it was "so strange and bizarre." The creature, however, had been reported by others on several occasions and was believed to have inhabited a tin cow barn that was a ruin remaining from the Belcoville munitions plant.

It was reported that, at around the time of the alleged sightings, no animals would go near the old barn and that "the floor of the cow barn and the cow barn itself . . . were always clean," as if someone, or something, lived there and maintained it.

Over the past few years, however, the surrounding field seems to have been repopulated by animals and there have been no more Monkey-Man sightings. Locals believe that the creature has died.

Moving on from Monkey-Men, we find that bizarre big birds have also made their presence known in New Jersey from time to time. During the week of January 9, 1909, the same week that Jersey Devil mania gripped south Jersey, another demonic creature was sighted near Asbury Park. An article in the Asbury Park *Evening Press* related that Dan Possack of Millville had an encounter with "one of the strangest freaks of nature, or a monster straight from the bad place," while doing his chores in his backyard.

According to the article, Possack reported that he heard someone in the yard calling out to him. He turned and saw "a monster beast-bird" approximately eighteen feet tall. The creature asked him in perfect English where the garbage can was! Understandably frightened, Possack ran toward his barn but the bird intercepted him and wrapped its red beak around the man's body. Possack started to hit it with the ax that he wore on his belt.

Even more bizarrely, Possack was dumbfounded to find that he was able to chop splinters out of the big bird's body, as though it were made of wood. At the same time, the creature whispered something unintelligible into his ear, apparently annoying Possack enough that he chopped with his ax directly into the beast's face. As the article continued, "Out popped an eyeball, and with a scream of pain, the assailant took in a long breath, filled its body like a balloon, and floated into space."

Reports don't get much stranger than that. One's first inclination is to wonder what the man had been drinking or smoking, but Possack swore it was all true. And that was not the only birdlike beast that has flapped its way across New Jersey.

In 1966, during a UFO flap in Wanaque, at least one witness encountered a very strange creature near a pond. "Fred A." reported this many years later:

> During the seventh grade, I had a science project to identify and categorize as many insects as I could

> find. . . . With my trusty net and killing jar, I traveled to my destination and got down to business. Not ten minutes into my endeavor, I noticed this huge shadow moving back and forth across the pond. I looked up and saw the biggest, scariest birdlike creature with glaring eyes gliding silently across the pond. It looked like it had fur rather than feathers, and its wingspan was about twenty feet. I beat a hasty retreat.

This particular encounter begs the question, was there a connection between the UFO sightings and this strange creature? And if so, what was it? We may never have the answer.

From big birds to big cats: cougars, panthers, and pumas have been seen in New Jersey as well. A gentleman known as "Hank S.," who lives in New Milford, less than 30 miles from the center of New York City, reported a sighting on the *Cryptozoology* Web site in March 2009. "The last wild cougar killed in NJ was in the mid-1800s. But slowly and incrementally apocryphal accounts of cougars have been creeping in," he wrote. "Now my daughter is one of those who had a sighting."

Hank S. went on to report that his daughter "and several of the neighbor kids have seen a cougar lying down on a rock watching them." Officially, the New Jersey Department of Fish and Wildlife denies that there are any cougars in the Garden State. The animal control officer in West Milford backed that claim, according to Hank, telling him "There are no mountain lions in New Jersey!"

While one may wonder why a mountain lion would be roaming such a populated area, Hank S. has his own theory:

> Did I mention that the Town has several enormous reservoirs in it? Due to 9/11 there are now protected

> areas that border all reservoirs in the USA. These areas have essentially returned to their wild state and harbor an abundance (and in West Milford's case) an over-abundance of fauna.

On May 1, 2006, Monmouth County police were investigating a series of sightings of a large, black, mysterious mountain lion or some kind of phantom panther around Dutch Lane, along the Colts Neck–Marlboro border.

Conservation officials during that 2006 flap studied a large paw print and took scat back for analysis. The New Jersey State Division of Fish and Wildlife confirmed the paw print did come from a large cat, but they were not clear if the print belonged to a mountain lion.

Certainly there has been an increase in phantom panther reports in recent years. Take for instance the black panther seen in and around Vineland, starting on April 28, 2007. Many local residents observed it, and after a news report appeared on local television on April 30, police headquarters was deluged with calls. More than thirty people dialed in saying they had seen the animal in April.

Eyewitnesses claimed the cat was the size of a German shepherd. Some people believed the cat to be 20 to 30 pounds, while others estimated they saw an animal that must have been more than 80 pounds. One eyewitness, Vineland resident Zoe Paraskevas, was sure she saw something huge.

"Panthers are not native to New Jersey. But I suppose anything is possible," said Department of Environmental Protection spokesperson Darlene Yuhas. "We are not taking the report lightly, but at this point there's nothing that tells us there's a panther in the area." During the spring of 2009, the explosion of reports was so great that even *The New Yorker*, on June 8, 2009, published in their famed "Talk of the Town," a level-headed and insightful column by Nick Paumgarten, entitled

"Suburban Legends: Panther(S)!" on cryptic large cats being reported in the Palisades of New Jersey. One resident who knew the renowned tracking guru Tom Brown Jr. was able to get the assistance of a Brown acolyte named Shane Hobel. Hobel went to a construction site where the mystery cat had been seen and the first cat tracks were found just south of the lot. A crewmember there was grading gravel.

"You guys looking for the phantom panthers?" one of the construction workers said to Hobel.

According to Paumgarten, "Hobel replied that the panthers were not phantoms. The man said, 'People actually saw them? Did they have a couple of cocktails in 'em?' Hobel laughed politely and then dropped into a thicket off the road."

But there may be even stranger catlike creatures in New Jersey. On April 24, 2003, a young man named "Justin" posted a report to the *Cryptozoology* Web site that was very weird indeed. Under the heading, "Strange Humanoid-Faced and Legged Cat-like Creature Sighted in NJ," he wrote that in June or July of 2001, he and his friend Alex had been on a bike ride by the Barnegat Lighthouse. They turned to ride back up Third Street, where a number of cats had congregated. Most of them scattered as the young boys rode by when Justin saw something that he took to be a cat at first, but turned out to be something quite different:

> Right there laying in the middle of the blacktop driveway was this creature. . . . It had cat-sized body proportions (two and a half to three feet from head to tail), but the tail was like a ferret's . . . the head and face was more monkey-like/humanoid-like, I think . . . its face was hairless. Its fur was brownish, I think. Also, it didn't have hindquarters like a cat or rabbit would have. It had humanoid legs.

Apparently, the face was so humanoid that Justin recalled this:

> It noticed my shock. It looked at me like it knew it was doing something wrong. . . . It then stood up, turned. I noticed its tail went down at a forty-five degree angle. . . . (It) hopped into the bushes on the left side of the driveway. I then heard it run away into the backyard.

Unfortunately, Justin's friend didn't see the creature. The writer ended his account by opining, "I don't believe this thing is an inbred cat or fox. It recognized my shock. I believe this creature is intelligent."

St. Joseph's Church on Pavonia Avenue in Jersey City has its own strange entity. For the past eighty years or so, two unexplained lights that locals call "St. Joseph's Cat's Eyes" have peered out from the church's belfry. According to the book *Weird N.J.*, they are said to be "pale, phosphorescent, glimmering, shaped like half moons, and at times (they) show a bloody red streak."

No one in Jersey City seems to know what causes these lights, although thousands of people have seen them since they first appeared in July 1921; at that time, five thousand onlookers were fascinated by them.

Priests have tried to find the source of the "eyes." They even sprinkled flour onto the belfry floor to see if whatever was up there would leave footprints, but none were ever found.

In 1954, the "eyes" made a dramatic and eerie reappearance after a sexton was found dead in the choir loft. The last words he was known to have uttered were "I'm going into the belfry." The mysterious "cat's eyes" then appeared, off and on, for the next three weeks.

A journalist by the name of Matthew F. Amato Jr. saw the phenomenon in 1991. He reported his encounter in *Weird N.J.*:

> When I was a senior news columnist, I was sent out on assignment with our photographer to view the St. Joseph's Cats Eyes for the first time since 1954. On February 27, 1991, standing on the northwest corner of Baldwin Avenue and Newark Avenue in front of the luncheonette, right across from the Brennan Courthouse, I saw the eyes again. That night, I did all I could to see if the eyes were a reflection of lights from the courthouse or anywhere else. I could find no possible reflection from anywhere. I showed my father a photograph, and he just shook his head in amazement, as these were the eyes he failed to see in 1954.

There are some sightings of New Jersey cryptids that defy easy categorization. Could there be mystery kangaroos hopping about the state? On December 15, 1925, the *Daily Times* noted that a strange animal had been shot while stealing chickens from a farm in Greenwich. The befuddled farmer supposedly showed the carcass to dozens if not hundreds of visitors (no photograph was published), but no one could come up with a reasonable theory about what it was. It was described as being the size of a grown Airedale, but when alive, it had hopped about like a kangaroo. Its front was higher off the ground than its rear and it crouched on its hind feet, which had four webbed toes. Its eyes were supposedly yellow.

Sadly, this was another story that was never investigated further. It became another footnote to be tucked away in the miscellaneous cryptid files.

Another weird beast had been seen the previous year in West Orange. According to a report in the *New York Herald* on July 3, 1924, Mrs. Clyde Vincent, a local resident, had a chance encounter with something she had never seen before. Mrs. Vincent described the incident: "We were picnicking along the road a while ago when an animal that had a head like a deer, that ran like a rabbit, and that had fiery eyes came along and jumped all over us."

While one person reporting such a creature may inspire an investigator to ask her how much she had been drinking at this picnic, there was corroborating evidence supplied by other eyewitnesses. A policeman on duty reported seeing the same creature and a farmer in nearby Livingston had seen it "jumping about his fields." The police thought the animal may have been a kangaroo that had escaped from a circus, but when they checked into it, they found that there had been no circuses nearby, and no escaped kangaroos.

Another very strange creature sighting was recently reported on an anomalistic Web site. Under the heading "Strange Creature in New Jersey," the anonymous witness, who lives in Bergen County in north Jersey, recalled something very strange that she had seen when she was thirteen years old (the witness was 38 at the time of writing):

> I was in the kitchen and it was a summer night. The sky had just become dark. My mother was giving my brother a haircut in the other room. I was alone in the kitchen. I heard a strange high-pitched squeak outside the kitchen door. I felt the hair on the back of my neck stand up. It was not a sound I ever heard before.

The witness went on to open the side door and go outside into the gathering darkness.

> There on the pavement was a creature that stood about three and a half feet tall. It was fat, furry, brown in color and stood up on its two hind legs and had short front paws. It had red swirling eyes that were totally hypnotic. It had a wide mouth filled with sharp teeth that went straight across its face. I froze in full terror. I had the feeling that this thing could move extremely fast and it was going to tear me to pieces.

Although in a state of panic, the witness managed to open the door and run screaming into the house. By the time the rest of the family came out to see the weird little beastie, it had vanished. The witness never saw it again.

There was more to the story, however. The writer's sister, who was fifteen years older, claimed that when she was four years old and playing in the basement of the same house, she had seen a similar creature. She and her sibling decided to draw what they had seen, separately from each other, and when they compared drawings, found that they were exactly the same. There was still more:

> After all those years I now live in the same house, but with my daughter now. My daughter has been telling me she has been hearing a strange sound outside her window on and off for a little over a year. . . . One night last year I was up late (1:30 A.M.) and she came to my room and said, "I hear it, mom. Come to my room!" Sure enough, I heard it too. It had that same weird sound that I had heard years ago, but this time slightly different. I couldn't see anything, but I stood by the

> window for over a half hour that night listening in shock to this creature. I could only explain the sound as a scream that was unearthly and bone-chilling. A sound something like screeching metal and animals dying combined. But it was unnaturally loud as if it was amplified!

What could these strange entities be? There are no easy answers, but in New Jersey, even in highly populated areas, there seem to be more than a few "long-legged beasties and things that go bump in the night."

Cape May Sea Serpent and Marine Monsters

Being so open to the sea makes the Jersey shoreline an obvious playground for marine monsters. A 30-foot sea-monster caught in Raritan Bay in 1822 is widely believed to have been a basking shark. This species is often blamed for being beached sea serpents, but something else altogether appeared to be happening directly off the coast of New Jersey for most of the last half of the nineteenth century. Indeed, one of the most famous marine monsters in the area was called the Cape May Sea Serpent, or more casually, His Lordship.

There have been several sightings of this beast through the years. On April 20, 1855, the *New York Times* reported that a dispatch dated April 19 received in Philadelphia from Cape May said "a Sea Serpent, one hundred feet long, was seen there." The article noted that a $1,000 reward was being offered to apprehend the creature and an expedition was already pursuing it. The article also reported that the serpent had been previously spotted in the same area the year before.

On March 30, 1883, the schooner *Annie L. Hall* sighted what looked like a capsized ship on the Grand Banks in the North Atlantic Ocean. It turned out, however, to be a turtle, "40 feet long, 30 feet wide, and 30 feet from the apex of the back to the bottom of the under shell." The flippers were 20 feet long. Captain W. L. Green and some fishermen off Long Branch apparently confused this report in contemporary newspapers with a more conventional 100-foot-long sea monster sighting that took place in November 1883.

Two men saw a sea serpent near Kingston Point, on the Hudson River, in August 1886. It was seen swimming in the freshwater, at the mouth of the river where it interacts with the ocean. The reports continued into the twentieth century. In November 1921, a 15-ton beast washed ashore at Cape May. Based on the rather long history of sea serpents off New Jersey, sometimes people just can't help themselves, however. A story reported in the July 5, 1934, edition of the *New Jersey Courier* noted that Frank Freeman, the general manager of the Phipps Estate, was sitting in his Island Beach home on a foggy Sunday afternoon when a "monstrous shape" emerged from the water just outside his living room window.

Freeman called, or rather "yelled," to his wife, who entered the room and promptly screamed when she saw the "monster writhing just a few yards away." Freeman ran from the house, suddenly recalling that he had given some officers from the Lakehurst Naval Air Station permission to have a picnic on the beach. He had "ghastly visions of the serpent devouring part of the Navy while they were swimming."

When he reached the picnic grounds, he ran toward the group, which included not only officers, but their wives and children as well. To his horror, he saw the monster near the beach, "leering maliciously with shining eyes." He actually thought he saw smoke emanating from its nostrils. But then he turned and saw one Lt. Cmdr. Reichelder "fondling the monster, pulling playfully on its tongue."

Freeman also saw Comdr. C. E. Rosandahl leaning up against a tree, convulsed with laughter, and Lt. Comdr. G. H.

Mills, "rolling in the dirt and violently laughing." It had all been a joke, and the joke was on Freeman.

The "serpent" was dragged up onshore and revealed to be "odd pieces of rubberized cloth discarded from blimps and balloons" that had been pieced together by members of the dirigible crew. "Thus ended the tale of the sea serpent of Barnegat Bay."

Well, the Barnegat Bay sea serpent may have been a hoax, but fossil records show that sea serpents did indeed once inhabit the shores of New Jersey. In fact, the gigantic Mosasaurus, once considered the longest of all known marine reptiles, slithered under the waters of the state in the Cretaceous Period. E. D. Cope wrote in *The American Naturalist* in 1870, "Ten species of this group are known from the Cretaceous beds of the United States, of which six have been found in New Jersey." He wrote, "In relative abundance of individuals, as well as of species, New Jersey is much in advance of any other part of the world where excavations have been made."

The Mosasaurus was a 60-foot nightmare, "literally a living pillar towering above waves or brush of the shore swamps." As a predator, it was at the very top of the prehistoric food chain. Could individuals of this species have survived into the present day? If so, this survival could account for the many sea serpent sightings near the Jersey Shore.

Prehistoric creatures are one thing, but what about the the headline "Mermaid Found in New Jersey," as proclaimed in New York's Port Jervis *Evening Gazette* on August 10, 1869? Consider this news report:

> The people of Tom's River, N.J., are just now having a little sensation—it being nothing less than the capture of a veritable mermaid or at least a water animal strongly

> resembling that poetic species of fish. Two fishermen, while pursuing their vocation a few days ago in the Inlet, affected the capture after a violent struggle. At seeing the animal its captors became hugely frightened, and took to their heels. After a while they mustered up sufficient courage to return and look at their prize. In appearance it more resembled a human being than a fish, having a face frightfully like that of a man or woman, with body and breasts exactly resembling the latter. The lower part terminated in a fish tail. The fishermen, after looking at the monster, became so superstitious, that they threw it back into the sea. It's a pity they did not preserve it.

As to what the New Jersey lake, river, and creek monsters are, well, that's an entirely different kettle of fish.

Lake Hopatcong Horror and Other Freshwater Weirdies

Nestled in the mountains of northern New Jersey on the border between Sussex and Morris counties lies Lake Hopatcong, the largest freshwater body of water in the state. Roughly four square miles in area, the lake used to be separated into two parts, the Great Pond and the Little Pond. The lake was enlarged in the eighteenth century when a dam was built in the Musconetong River on its southern end. The water level was raised by six feet as the two lakes became one.

Before European settlers arrived, Lenape Indians lived near the shores of the lake. Theirs was a good life: Lake Hopatcong, then as now, was home to a huge variety of game fish, including trout, largemouth bass, perch, eels, and herring, and perhaps something else.

The story goes that roughly two hundred years ago, a strange and immense beast that lived in the lake terrorized early settlers and Native Americans alike. The creature supposedly had a gigantic horselike head, antlers or horns, and a body roughly the size and texture of an elephant's. Whenever it surfaced, it would do so with a tremendous splash and terrify the residents on the shore.

At some point, the monster was seen no more, and the Indians told the settlers that it had fallen through the ice that covered the lake in winter and had drowned in the freezing water. A few of the settlers got together in a rowboat and went out to the area where the Lenapes said the creature had gone through the ice, and sure enough, when they returned to shore, they reported that they had seen the beast's body lying at the bottom of the lake, its titanic skull and 10-foot-long antlers plainly visible from the surface.

But the beast may not be dead after all, or perhaps its offspring now inhabit the lake. According to a young man who called himself "Pete" in the book *Weird NJ*, something large and strange still lurks beneath the surface of Lake Hopatcong. Pete wrote that something very unsettling happened to him and a friend on November 11, 1999:

> My friend and I went to Lake Hopatcong to pull my boat out of the water, and you wouldn't believe what we saw! It was a pitch-black wave that was six or seven feet tall. When it hit our dock, it almost knocked us off it! Then we saw something go up and down. We thought it was a buoy, but my neighbor said it was too big for a buoy. My friend fell off the deck and into the lake. He popped up about ten feet away and said he felt something grab him.

Despite the beast's rather scary reputation, most residents around Lake Hopatcong today look at it with a sort of affection. Fondly known as "Hoppie," the beast has become a kind of mascot for the local tourist industry. The Landing Web site at landingnewjersey.com notes that the town "has a population of approximately 7,300 people, several dozen white-tailed deer, a few bears, and one elusive water creature named 'Hoppie,' who lives in the depths of Lake Hopatcong and can occasionally be seen swimming on the surface of the lake." It goes on to remind visitors not to "think of him as a sea monster," because "he is generally considered to be quite friendly!"

The real monster in the lake may now be vegetable rather than animal. In the *New Jersey Real-Time News* of August 2, 2009, an article by Katherine Santiago was headlined, "Weeds Snarl Lake Hopatcong," and went on to describe "an underwater mountain of weeds that are choking the health from Lake Hopatcong." Perhaps Hoppie has swum off to less-green pastures?

But another true monster was recently photographed at Lake Hopatcong. The headline of the *Courier Post* of February 23, 2010, read, "Man Pulls Monster Musky from Lake Hopatcong," and the article by Adam Monacelli was accompanied by a photo of a 46-inch musky that fisherman John Wilhelm had pulled from the lake. He and a friend had been ice fishing on the lake when he caught the 26-pound fish. "I was shocked," he said. "The eyeballs were larger than a quarter and it had teeth like a pit bull. The teeth are three quarters of an inch long."

Wilhelm let the huge fish go after measuring, weighing, and photographing it. "We absolutely threw it back," he said. "Catch and release—something that big and beautiful should go back in the lake."

Perhaps something "that big and beautiful" could be food for something even bigger, though perhaps not so beautiful?

But Hoppie isn't the only underwater beast to swim its way through New Jersey. There's also "Tommy," the shadowy denizen of the Toms River, a freshwater river and estuary about 19 miles long that winds its way through Ocean County. The river's source is in the Pine Barrens of the northern part of the county; the river flows southeast, winding through wetland areas and ultimately into Barnegat Bay in the Atlantic Ocean.

The river has a somewhat controversial history. It was known as Goose Creek until it was renamed in the early eighteenth century by one of three people. Some say it was named for an English captain named William Toms, while others claim it actually received its moniker from farmer and ferryman Thomas Luker. But the most popular story has it that a Native American named Tom, or "Indian Tom," as locals christened him, is the person for whom the waterway was named.

Whatever the case, the legend of Tommy, an underwater creature seen by inhabitants along the river, dates back to precolonial times. There's even an unsubstantiated rumor that Tommy sank a boat on the river in the 1920s. Supposedly, Tommy can often be glimpsed from the gazebo in Island Heights, "when the full moon is directly overhead." As "David K." wrote in *Weird NJ*, residents gather in the summer to light a bonfire on Summit Beach in Island Heights "to send Tommy a message. They only hope he doesn't claim another victim."

Where the river flows into the ocean at Barnegat Bay, there are famous sea serpents, as we saw in the last chapter. Could these be relatives of or Tommy himself, having a frolic in the sea?

Other strange freshwater cryptids seem to be about, too. Cryptozoologist Mark A. Hall reported in his article, "Sobering Sights of Pink Unknowns," in *Wonders* of December 1992, that Ivan T. and Sabina Sanderson observed a long, pinkish-orange, worm-like animal in a deep pond on his Columbia farm around 1971. Loren Coleman in his 1983 book *Mysterious America* mentioned the monster of North Shrewsbury River.

Finally, Roy P. Mackal, in his 1980 book *Searching for Hidden Animals*, told of the monster reported on March 1, 1975, in the Old Mill Pond, near Trenton.

While there is no monster associated with it, the Blue Hole, located in the dense woods near Monroe in Gloucester County, has an eerie atmosphere all its own. Local parents warn their children not to swim there, for there are tales of mysterious "whirlpools" (some say "creatures" or the Jersey Devil) that suck people down to a watery doom.

It's one of those ponds that are alleged to be bottomless, although those who believe there is a bottom say it is made of quicksand. Circular and some 70 feet across, the Blue Hole was actually a popular picnic and swimming area in the 1930s, but a storm washed out a bridge spanning the Great Egg Harbor River in the 1960s, and now it can only be reached on foot.

The color that gives the Blue Hole its name is highly unusual for the area, as most lakes and ponds in these pinelands are a muddy brown color due to the large deposits of iron, sediment, and tannic acid. Its bright blue water seems out of place, shining like a jewel in the dark forest.

There are numerous tales of how the Blue Hole came to be created. There are those who say it is the result of a meteor striking the earth, leaving a crater that was filled in by water. Others say that it's a "pingo," a small body of water created during the last ice age. Whatever the case, it's a one-of-a-kind body of water in New Jersey.

The water has warm spots and cold spots, averaging between 58 to 60 degrees Fahrenheit all year round. These anomalies make it easy to understand why people became afraid of the Blue Hole after the area was abandoned in the '60s. And there are still those who say that something pulls people down into that shiny blue water, and that those who dare to swim there may not live to regret it; they'll just be the latest victims of whatever lurks in the Blue Hole.

There is at least one fully documented case of an all-too-real water monster in New Jersey, the Matawan Man-Eater. It began on an oppressively hot July 1 in the humid summer of 1916. The heat had already been blamed for one death in Jersey City. There was no air conditioning back then and the summer had been brutal to both individuals and businesses.

The tourist season was at its height in Beach Haven, where everyone was in the water trying to escape from the heat and humidity. It seemed like a typical day for that summer until young Penn graduate Charles E. Van Sant screamed for help. Van Sant, a Beach Haven resident, had swum out about 100 yards before he decided to make his way back to shore, leisurely swimming and riding the waves. He got to within 50 feet of the shore when some other swimmers in shallower water noticed a large shadow following behind him. They shouted to him, but he didn't hear them. Then he felt something take hold of his legs.

Lifeguard Alexander Ott, a former Olympic swimmer, saw Van Sant suddenly vanish beneath the waves. Immediately afterwards, the water turned red.

Ott jumped into the water and swam to the spot where he had last seen the swimmer. As he arrived near where the water was stained crimson, he saw the telltale fin and the dark body of the thing that had attacked Van Sant.

Ott found Van Sant, covered in blood and unconscious, and pulled him back to shore. The lifeguard did his best to stop the bleeding, but it was hopeless. Van Sant's legs had been horribly mutilated, and the hapless swimmer died from wounds inflicted by the shark.

Needless to say, this horrifying story made all the newspapers, both locally and nationally, but local scientists wrote off the incident as a one-time freak accident. There had never before been any reports of shark attacks in New Jersey waters. Some experts of the time even insisted that sharks didn't attack living people and that Van Sant was only "accidentally" attacked by a shark that mistook him for a floating corpse. Unfortunately, we didn't know as much about sharks then as we do now. The scientists were fatally incorrect.

Five days later, the Fourth of July holiday was in full swing, and tourists descended upon the Jersey shore by the hundreds. There had been no more shark sightings, and those who ran the seasonal businesses on the shore felt they had been given a reprieve.

July 6, however, was a turning point. Spring Lake was a town about 20 miles north of Beach Haven; there, near the Essex and Sussex Hotel, a twenty-seven-year-old bellboy named Charles Bruder went for a swim on his day off. It was the last swim he would ever take.

Bruder had swum past the lifelines when suddenly he vanished beneath the water. A woman on shore pointed to the spot where Bruder had disappeared and shouted, "The man in the red canoe is upset!" But there was no red canoe. The red spot she pointed to was blood.

Lifeguards took to the water in a rescue boat. When they reached the scene of carnage, they saw Bruder's arm protruding above the waves. As they pulled him from the water, it seemed as though his body was extremely light. When they got him onto the boat, they saw why. There was very little left of him below the waist.

"Shark bit me!" Bruder screamed. "Bit my legs off!" Those were his final words.

Col. William Gray Schauffler, Surgeon General of the New Jersey National Guard, confirmed what had happened to Bruder. In his report, he wrote, "There is not the slightest doubt that a man-eating shark inflicted the injuries."

The hysteria began. Now people were seeing sharks all along the Jersey coast. On July 8, the resort town of Asbury Park installed mesh and metal nets along the beach to protect the public.

At the same time, more foolishness about sharks came from the mouths of so-called experts. Dr. Frederick Lucas, director of the Museum of Natural History in Manhattan, disagreed with Colonel Schauffler regarding Charles Bruder's death. He stated flatly, "A shark's jaw is simply not powerful enough to do that kind of damage." Between such ill-founded opinions and the metal nets on the shore, many swimmers felt that it was safe to go back into the water again.

No one in the town of Matawan, 30 miles up the coast, expected to have anything to worry about from sharks. Matawan was 11 miles inland from the ocean and here the only swimming spots available were in the Matawan Creek, a small tidal creek that emptied out into the bay.

It was mid-morning on July 12, another hot and humid day; the temperature was approaching 90 degrees when retired fishing boat captain Thomas Cattrell decided to take a break from the heat at his bait and tackle shop near the mouth of the Matawan Creek. When he crossed over the new trolley drawbridge, he noticed something strange in the water below him. He saw a large shadow there, and he literally couldn't believe his eyes. But as a professional fisherman, he knew what he was seeing: a large shark, approximately 10 feet in length, was swimming upstream.

Cattrell shouted to two workmen on the drawbridge, pointing out the shark in the creek, but the creature was already out of their line of vision. Then he ran back to his shop to phone the nearby town of Keyport, which was in the direction that the shark had been heading. Then Cattrell ran to Matawan, which was also upstream, to warn the townspeople there.

Despite his shrill warnings, few people believed what Cattrell told them. They were aware of the other shark attacks—who wasn't?—but they had a hard time believing that a shark would be swimming up a freshwater creek. Captain Cattrell's warnings fell on deaf ears, with most townspeople assuming both the heat and the shark panic that had been spreading across New Jersey had affected him. Ignoring Captain Cattrell's warnings would prove to be another fatal mistake. That day, twelve-year-old Lester Stillwell and four of his friends decided to go for a swim in the Matawan Creek. He had been given the afternoon off from the Anderson Saw Mill, where he worked with his father; this, of course, was before the advent of child labor laws. Because of the oppressive heat, the mill closed down that afternoon.

The five boys splashed in the water, and Stillwell told them to watch him as he floated on his back. One of his friends, Charles Van Brunt, saw something large move past him in the water towards Stillwell. Almost immediately, Stillwell was pulled forcefully beneath the surface. Van Brunt could see the white underbelly and gleaming fangs of the shark, which rolled about in the water as its jaws snapped shut around Stillwell's body. The boy bobbed up and down, filling the water with blood as the shark tore him to pieces.

His friends got out of the reddened creek as fast as they could and ran to Main Street, screaming for help. They were heard by, among other people, Watson Stanley Fisher, who owned and operated a dry cleaning and tailor shop. As soon as he heard the ghastly news, he closed his shop and met up with two of his friends, George Burlew and Arthur Smith.

At first, they thought perhaps Stillwell had been the victim of an epileptic seizure and that the boys had imagined the rest. Nevertheless, he and his friends agreed that the boy would have to be rescued from the creek regardless of what had happened to him. Captain Cattrell was on the scene as well. By this time, he was piloting a motorboat.

Meanwhile, Smith, Fisher, and Burlew dove into the water, unaware that the shark was still attacking the boy's dead body. Just as Smith was about to give up the search, he felt something bump up against him in the water and, at the same time, saw that he was bleeding. A moment later, there was a scream from the area in which Fisher had last been seen. Fisher suddenly reappeared above the water and, according to journalist Floyd Gibbons quoting from George Burlew, "fought the fish like a madman, striking and kicking it with all his might. Three or four times during the struggle the shark pulled him under," he went on, "but each time he managed to get back to the surface. He seemed to be holding his own, but at best, it was an uneven battle. The shark was at home in the water—and Stanley wasn't."

Fisher ultimately broke free as the shark moved down the creek. Cattrell's motorboat reached him and he was pulled onboard. Most of the flesh was gone from his right leg. A tourniquet was quickly applied to the wound, but it had little more effect than a Band-Aid. Fisher was ultimately taken to Memorial Hospital in Long Branch.

The next morning, the Newark *Evening News* quoted Fisher: "I knew it was all up with me when I felt his grip on my thigh. It was an awful feeling. I can't explain it. Anyhow, I did my duty."

Fisher later died from loss of blood and shock as he was being taken into the operating room for surgery. But the Matawan Man-Eater's hunger had still not been sated.

The shark swam downstream, back toward the ocean, where it encountered four teenage boys from Cliffwood. They were swimming off the Wyckoff Dock. The boys were unaware of what had been going on upstream until someone onshore spotted them and screamed to them to get out of the creek.

The youngest boy, Joseph Dunn, felt something latch onto his leg as he was trying to get out of the water. Dunn's older brother Michael and the others tried to pull Joseph out of the creek. The boys grabbed Joseph by the arms as the shark continued to grasp its prey. Finally, the shark, its hunger apparently satiated at last, released Joseph and continued its swim back toward the ocean.

Joseph Dunn was one of the few who encountered the shark and lived to tell about it. The surgeons at St. Peter's Hospital in Brunswick even managed to save his leg and he was able to walk out of the hospital without the help of crutches.

In true horror movie fashion, however, the citizens of Matawan wanted revenge. Like the torch-wielding villagers in the old Universal monster movies, they demanded some kind of bloody satisfaction. The beast had left two dead and one injured. The shark itself was gone, although no one knew it at the time. But that didn't prevent the townspeople from unleashing their rage on something, anything.

For a full day, they vented their emotions on Matawan Creek. They dynamited it; they shot aimlessly into its depths. For twenty-four hours, the air and water were full of explosions. No one even knew what species of shark they were looking for. Blind justice was all they were after. They weren't even sure of its size, but it didn't matter. Dozens of sharks were slaughtered between the salt marsh and the ocean.

The bloated, dismembered corpse of Lester Stillwell floated to the surface two days after his horrible death, a few hundred yards upstream from where he had been attacked. Two railroad workers found it floating in Matawan Creek near a train trestle at 5:15 in the morning. When they saw the condition of the corpse—or what was left of it—the townspeople became even more enraged than they had been before.

Accounts vary as to who actually captured and killed the shark that had caused all the carnage. Some say it was a fisherman by the name of Michael Schleisser, who caught the creature near Raritan Bay. It was a 9-foot-long great white shark, and when it was dissected, fifteen pounds of dismembered limbs, bone, and other human remains were supposedly found within it.

The other account, however, is perhaps more satisfying and offers a bit more closure. It holds that the same Captain Cattrell who had warned the populace about the beast in the first place captured the shark. Once he netted it and killed it, he displayed the Matawan Beast to the public, charging more than three thousand people ten cents a head to see its corpse. Whether it was really the shark that had attacked the citizens of Matawan was an open question, but it seemed to satisfy the onlookers.

The real closure came when funeral services were held for Stillwell and Fisher. The latter's service was held at the Arrowsmith Funeral Home on Main Street in Matawan, while Stillwell's was held at his parents' home. Dozens, if not hundreds, of people attended the ceremonies. Both victims were interred at Rose Hill Cemetery in Matawan.

It was now obvious to all that a single shark had been responsible for every fatality and mutilation that had occurred along the Jersey coast and in Matawan that summer. It seemed unimaginable, but it was apparently true, and no one had any really convincing theories as to why one shark would have gone on a rampage.

Other sharks were sighted along the New Jersey coast in that bloody summer of 1916, and some were even captured and killed by fishermen. The hysteria eventually died down and the sharks themselves seemed to tire of the area. By then it was too late to save the tourist season. The events, however, later served as inspiration for Peter Benchley's book *Jaws*, which spawned a major motion picture in 1975.

Lizardmen and Various Vicious Reptilians

Lizardmen in New Jersey? The record for such creatures in the state is minor and cannot compare with the overwhelming series of stories issuing from the Ohio River Valley. But when you least expect them, for you may try to avoid and ignore them, they will sneak up on you. Every few years, the strange Lizardmen and other reptilian accounts continue to dot the bottom of the inside pages of the region's newspapers. Nowadays, they are popping up as almost overlooked weird weblog stories and on the local television news broadcasts from the state.

One of the most famed cases of these reptilians in modern times was the Lizard Man of Scape Ore Swamp in Lee County, South Carolina. The encounter involved a 7-foot-tall, bipedal, three-toed, three-fingered, scaly beast attacking seventeen-year-old Chris Davis while he was changing a tire early on the morning of June 30, 1988. A series of long scratches were later found on the roof of Davis's car. Davis became an international celebrity as a teenager when he reported the first sighting of the legendary Lizard Man. New Jersey has its Lizardmen reports too. You can take the reports, tales, and sightings of these curious creatures and draw a continuous watery line down the Susquehanna River through the southern tier of New York State, into the Tamarack swamps along the Delaware, and ending in the counties of Morris and Sussex in New Jersey. Take a map out and look at what you'll find there. Places where no one wants to live. Now you know why.

During the summer of 1973, residents of the Newton-Lafayette area in New Jersey described a giant, manlike alligator they had seen locally. Newspaper reporters wrote about an old Indian tale from the region of a giant, man-sized fish that could never be caught. The interplay between what is being seen in New Jersey and the reports from the nearby Empire State is strong. In 1977, New York State conservation naturalist Alfred Hulstruck reported that the state's southern tier had "a scaled, manlike creature [that] appears at dusk from the red, algae-ridden waters to forage among the fern and moss-covered uplands."

Not all the reptilian creatures in New Jersey are manlike. On September 22, 1895, Willard P. Shaw and his family and neighbors saw a huge snake off their front porch at Spring Lake. It appeared to be 75 to 100 feet long, with its head sticking 6 feet out of the water. The head was flat with a gatorlike snout. It moved about 40 miles an hour with up-and-down writhing movements.

Alligators in the sewers are said to exist in New York City—and in out-of-place locations in New Jersey, as Loren Coleman detailed in *Mysterious America*, with good records from the 1930s onward. Such cases continue right up to modern times.

In New Jersey, for example, some kind of creature had been seen for more than three weeks in a pond in Trenton's Stacy Park, before it was captured on September 2, 2009.

Linda DiPiano, a state wildlife biologist, took custody of a 4-foot alligator that had been lured into a dog cage that contained a chicken leg and thigh. News helicopters hovered in the airspace above the backyard of Edwin Gonzalez, where officials held the alligator inside a cage.

"Since the sighting several weeks ago, we have checked our [traps] every hour starting at about 6:30 in the morning. I wasn't expecting a phone call, but when it came I rushed right over here," said an official. "We rowed out toward the cage and then I saw the alligator's head pop up inside the cage. It was pretty exciting, of course, something that nobody at Animal Control had ever been involved in."

Gonzalez said, "The alligator has been eluding us for some time, so to row up to the cage and see it there was pretty cool. Luckily, this ends with us safely catching the alligator and nobody getting hurt." He added, "The way these people are hanging around this alligator, I guess you could say it's become a celebrity."

The Ultimate New Jersey Monster

We come to the end of our exploration of the monsters of New Jersey, well aware that the state has given us no clear-cut creatures and cryptids that are easy to catalogue, just as we promised. As we near the final words of this book, however, we must celebrate the remarkable invention and contribution to cryptozoology of one man. You can choose which one it ultimately is, the psychologist or the drunk or perhaps both.

Leonard George, born in 1957, is based in Vancouver, British Columbia, and is best known for his writing and lectures on varieties of anomalous phenomena, spirituality, psychology, and history. George is a clinical psychologist, writer, lecturer, and occasional broadcaster; his official academic affiliations include Capilano University, the University of British Columbia, and the Psychology Clinic at Simon Fraser University. He has offered seminars across North America and Europe. He earned his BS at the University of Toronto and his MA and PhD at the University of Western Ontario. His research focuses on historical and philosophical aspects of psychology, anomalistic and health psychology, psychology and the arts, and schizophrenia. His other interests include writing, fitness, and meditation, as well as the finer and the stranger things in life.

George is the author of two extensively annotated reference works on anomalistic experience and religious history. His attributed books include *Alternative Realities: The Paranormal, the Mystic, and the Transcendent in Human Experience* (New York: Facts on File, 1995) and *Crimes of Perception: An Encyclopedia of Heresies and Heretics* (New York: Paragon House, 1995). The latter work was included in the *Washington Post*'s 1995 roundup of notable religion-themed books.

If Leonard George is to be remembered for anything, it should be for a term that hits the name on the head and speaks to the topic and state that is the focus of this volume. George has coined the phrase *New Jersey Vegetable Monster*, which is today used by cryptozoologists and other researchers of anomalous phenomena and the unexplained to describe a sighting or incident that has exceptionally poor evidential support. He discusses the case on page 194 of his book, *Alternative Realities*.

According to George, the term originated with a sighting reported by a single severely intoxicated eyewitness, who claimed to have observed a humanoid resembling a giant stalk of broccoli. The original sighting, which allegedly occurred in the New Jersey Pine Barrens, was likely attributable to a case of delirium tremens.

The basis of the use of this expression today is that if something is so absurd and the eyewitness lacks almost any credibility, a cryptozoologist investigating this nearly completely unreliable sighting, out of no disrespect to other credible witnesses, may quietly slip the rejected case in his New Jersey Vegetable Monster file.

As in all investigations in New Jersey, as elsewhere, it is best to approach your quest with an open mind, critically, skeptically, and patiently.

APPENDIX

A Comprehensive List of Jersey Devil Sightings

The Devil Hunters, the official researchers of the Jersey Devil, on the Internet at njdevilhunters.com, via president and webmaster Laura K. Leuter, has kindly granted permission to publish a modified version of the group's chronological list of Jersey Devil sightings and encounters. You may contact Devil Hunters directly for more information about the Jersey Devil. We encourage people in New Jersey to support and meet other local researchers of established groups.

1735

Supposed birth year of the Jersey Devil, rumored to be named Smith J. Leeds.

1740

A priest exorcised the Jersey Devil for one hundred years after sighting the creature sporadically throughout 1735–40.

1800–20

Sometime between these dates, American naval hero Stephen Decatur sighted the creature and shot a hole through its wing.

1840

The Jersey Devil went on a rampage this year, and the state suffered a heavy loss of chickens and sheep. Note that this was the one hundredth anniversary of its exorcism.

1841

More livestock loss. People hear chilling screams and discover strange tracks. Local posses locate nothing.

1858

An article is published describing the fear in the residents of the Pine Barrens. They all seem hesitant to go out after dark, because of a winged beast roaming and terrorizing the woods.

1859

Jersey Devil sighted in Haddonfield.

1873–74

Seen in Bridgeton and Long Branch throughout the winter months.

1880s

Rumored to "carry off anything that moved" during this decade.

1894

Seen around Smithville, Long Beach Island, Brigantine Beach, Haddonfield, and Leeds Point.

1899

A big year. The Jersey Devil was accused of raiding the villages of Vincentown and Burrsville before heading up to New York. In New York, a man claimed to have heard ungodly screams and found he was missing sheep when he awoke the next morning. There were also reports of sightings of an unusual creature at Hyenga Lake, New York. The Jersey Devil then returned to New Jersey, where he would engage in his worst batch of terrorism yet.

SATURDAY, JANUARY 16–SUNDAY, JANUARY 17

- **Woodbury, NJ**

A man was leaving a hotel when he "heard a hissing" and saw something white flying across the street. "I saw two spots of phosphorus—the eyes of the beast. There was a white cloud, like escaping steam from an engine. It moved as fast as an auto."

- **Bristol, PA**

A man named John McOwen was awakened at 2 A.M. by the screams of his baby. He began hearing odd noises out in the backyard. The noises "sounded like the scratching of a phonograph before the music begins and yet it also had something of a whistle to it. You know how the factory whistle sounds? Well, it was something like that."

A police officer named James Sackville heard the neighborhood dogs suddenly begin to bark and growl uncontrollably. Sackville developed a strange feeling and instinctively turned around—and there, standing in the shadows, was the Jersey Devil. He said the creature had wings and hopped around and had the features of some peculiar animal he had never seen before. The voice of the creature was a horrible scream. Sackville began to run toward the creature, which turned and ran in retreat, screaming. Sackville fired his pistol, and the creature hovered above the ground before flying off into the dark night sky.

Bristol's postmaster, E. W. Minster, also had an encounter with the beast. He described it as follows:

> I awoke about two o'clock in the morning . . . and finding myself unable to sleep, I arose and wet my head with cold water as a cure for insomnia. As I got up, I heard an eerie, almost supernatural sound from the direction of the river. . . . I looked out upon the Delaware and saw flying diagonally across what appeared to be a large crane, but which was emitting a glow like a firefly. Its head resembled that of a ram, with curled horns, and its long thick neck was thrust forward in flight. It had long thin wings and short legs, the front legs shorter than the hind. Again, it uttered its mournful and awful call—a combination of a squawk and a whistle, the beginning very high and piercing and ending very low and hoarse.

Bristol residents awoke to find their yards covered with abnormal hoofprints.

- **Burlington, NJ**

Joseph Lowden and his family heard "noise, as of some heavy body trampling in the snow in the yard." The creature began circling the house and made an attempt to open the back door, and then left. Footprints were seen that night.

- **White City, NJ**

Two muskrat trappers encountered strange footprints.

- **Gloucester City, NJ**

James Fleson found eerie footprints in eight different yards, with a trail leading into a local junkyard. A Mrs. Shindle found hoofprints in her yard and said "It's a two-legged cow with wings."

MONDAY, JANUARY 18

- **Burlington, NJ**

The Lowden family awoke to find tracks from whatever had circled their house the night before. The snow had been packed down around the garbage can, with its contents half eaten and strewn across the ground. The residents of Burlington entered a state of panic, locking doors and windows, refusing to leave their homes, and staying in shock overnight. Practically every backyard in Burlington had been scarred with footprints. The prints were unbelievable—skipping from rooftop to rooftop, randomly vanishing, and leading into completely inaccessible areas. The size of the prints varied in each trail as well. Search posses formed and rewards were offered.

- **Columbus, Hedding, Kinkora, Rancocas**

Footprints were reported. Dogs refused to follow the trails.

TUESDAY, JANUARY 19

- **Gloucester City, NJ**

The Jersey Devil visited Mr. and Mrs. Nelson Evans at approximately 2:30 A.M. This is one of the most vivid and well-described sightings ever. Mr. Evans was awakened by strange noises. The couple stared out their bedroom window to watch the Jersey Devil standing on the roof of their shed for a full ten minutes. Mr. Evans gave the following description:

> It was about three feet and a half high, with a head like a collie dog and a face like a horse. It had a long neck, wings about two feet long, and its back legs were like those of a crane, and it had horse's hooves. It walked on its back legs and held up two short front legs with paws on them. It didn't use the front legs at all while we were watching. My wife and I were scared, I tell you, but I managed to open the window and say, "Shoo!" and it turned around, barked at me, and flew away.

Two professional muskrat hunters trailed the Jersey Devil for several miles. The tracks seemed to jump five-foot fences and squeeze under eight-inch spaces. One of the men claimed he would never leave his house without bringing his gun.

- **Camden, NJ**

A young girl fainted when she discovered strange tracks in the snow. The tracks appeared to be deformed, with one foot larger than the other. A sighting was reported, saying the creature looked "something like a possum, the size of a dog, with a shrill bark, flapping its wings and taking off into the air."

- **Swedesboro, NJ**

Another sighting, this time claiming that the creature had antlers or horns of some type.

- **Glassboro, NJ**

Reports of footprints came in. The prints had three toes and appeared slightly dog-like.

WEDNESDAY, JANUARY 20

- **Burlington, NJ**

A policeman saw the creature, whose "eyes were like blazing coals." The policeman was sure it was a "Jabberwocky."

- **Pemberton, NJ**

Rev. John Pursell saw the creature, stating he had "never seen anything like it before."

- **Haddonfield and Collingswood, NJ**

Search parties were created to locate the creature. They discovered strange tracks, which always seemed to disappear into thin air. The creature was seen in Collingswood, heading north towards Moorestown.

- **Moorestown, NJ**

John Smith saw the creature and chased it until it disappeared into a pit nearby. George Snyder also saw the creature, and the two described it as follows: "It was three feet high . . . long black hair over its entire body, arms and hands like a monkey, face like a dog, split hooves, and a tail a foot long."

- **Springside, NJ**

A trolley car operator saw a strange shape cross the tracks and then disappear into the shadows. He said, "It looked like a winged kangaroo with a long neck."

- **Riverside, NJ**

Ubiquitous tracks were made near chicken coops, buildings, and other structures. Joseph Mans found his puppy dead, surrounded by the strange tracks. The tracks appeared to be made by "small horse shoes" and were "everywhere, including the rooftop." Plaster casts were made from these prints.

THURSDAY, JANUARY 21

- **Camden, NJ**

A strange noise was heard at 1 A.M. at the Black Hawk Social Club. One of the members heard the noise at the back window and turned to find the beast staring in through the glass. The club members were immediately gripped with panic. The man attempted to scare the creature, which flew off screaming.

- **Haddon Heights, NJ**

A trolley passenger sighted the creature through a window at 2 A.M. The passengers all stared in horror as they watched the Jersey Devil flying near them. When the trolley car stopped, the creature circled above, screaming hissing noises before flying away. The conductor of the trolley, Lewis Boeger, gave this report:

> In general appearance it resembled a kangaroo. . . . It has a long neck and from what glimpse I got of its head its features are hideous. It has wings of a fairly good size and of course in the darkness looked black. Its legs are long and somewhat slender and were held in just such a position as a swan's when it is flying. We all tried to get a look at its feet to see what shape they were but the darkness was too great. It looked to be about four feet high.

- **Trenton, NJ**

William Cromley was returning home when his horse began to panic. When Cromley exited his buggy, he saw "quite a sight that froze the blood in his veins and caused his hair to stand upright." There before him stood a creature described as "a beast of fur and feathers, about the size of an average dog, with the face of a German shepherd, from which glowered large, sparkling eyes." The creature spread its wings and flew away.

E. P. Weeden, a Trenton councilman, was awakened by the sounds of someone attempting to break into his home. He ran to his windows and heard the sound of wings flapping. When he peered out his window, he saw hoofprints in the snow on his roof. These prints were found all over the town, including at the nearby arsenal.

- **Trenton and New Brunswick, NJ**

Trolleys in both cities maintained armed guards in case of a Jersey Devil attack.

- **Pitman, NJ**

Many poultry farms were missing large amounts of chickens.

- **Bridgeton and Millville, NJ**

Poultry men heard screeching cries and awoke to find some of their chickens were dead—without a single mark on them. The farmers all agreed that it was the work of the Jersey Devil.

- **Roebling, NJ**

Many more tracks were found covering a yard, looking as though an entire herd of creatures had come stampeding through the area overnight.

- **Burlington, NJ**

A woman heard a noise in the alley near her house at 6 A.M. Upon investigation, she found a creature with birdlike features and a horse's head. The creature appeared as if it were about to leap. The woman immediately shut the window and collapsed in fear. She said, "For some minutes I was so frightened I was unable to scream. My husband and son had already gone to work, and I was finally able to waken my youngest son, who was asleep upstairs." Although no one saw the creature in the alley again, there were small hoofprints covering the ground. Rumor had it that the mayor of Burlington ordered the police to shoot the creature on sight.

- **Leiperville, PA**

A man walking along a highway spotted the creature early in the morning, and claimed that it ran faster than the cars were driving. He described it as having "skin like an alligator, stood on its hind feet, and was about six feet tall."

- **Mount Holly, NJ**

William Cronk saw the creature flying across his yard, saying it looked like a crane. Job Shinn said it had "a horse-like head, long hind legs with claws, and big wings." He said it walked like a man and left tracks everywhere.

- **Clayton, NJ**

R. L. Campbell erroneously reported that the creature was dead after a man told him he had watched the creature walk towards an electric railway. The man said that the creature's tail had hit the rail line and suddenly there was a power surge and an explosion that melted tracks for twenty feet in both directions. They believed this to be the end of the creature, since no remains were found.

- **Atlantic City, NJ**

A telegraph lineman gave another account of the Jersey Devil being injured. His report was this:

> In an isolated spot in the Jersey Pines, about five miles from Pleasantville, at a place known as Beaver Pond, one of the linemen, Howard Campbell, was detailed on a piece of work a little distance from the rest of the men on duty. After walking a little way into the woods, his attention was attracted by something coming down the path toward him. He became so frightened by the unusual appearance of the thing that he straightway made for the nearest telegraph pole. Letting out several yells for help and losing his wits entirely by the time he reached the top of the pole, Campbell threw himself out on the mass of wires between the two poles and was lying there helpless by the time the rest of the gang, including myself, had arrived. Seeing the "Terror" on the pole, I raised my gun and fired. One shot broke a wing and it fell to the ground, uttering hideous screams; but before anyone could collect his wits the thing was up and off with long strides and a sort of hop, dragging one wing, and then disappearing into the pine thicket. We got ropes and other tackle and helped Campbell down from his precarious position. As nearly as I can

describe the terror, it had the head of a horse, the wings of a bat, and a tail like a rat's, only longer.

- **Philadelphia, PA**

Mrs. J. E. White was out in her backyard hanging laundry at approximately 4 P.M. in the afternoon when she noticed something sitting in a corner of her yard. Upon approaching the creature, it arose to six feet tall and revealed a body covered in scaly skin. White claimed the creature spurted flames from its mouth. White began screaming and collapsed. Her husband ran out just in time to catch a glimpse of the strange, frightening beast. Mr. White grabbed a support pole from the clothesline and swung it at the creature, until the creature finally escaped and flew off.

Right after that incident, a driver reported almost hitting the creature as it scrambled across the road. Another man, William Becker, claimed to have thrown stones at the Jersey Devil. Another man claimed to have watched it sitting along the roadside.

- **Westville, NJ**

Two women at a meeting glanced out the window to see the strange thing sitting on the front lawn in the snow. The women canceled their meetings and called a few men to form a search party to find and destroy it.

- **West Collingswood, NJ**

Two men walking down a road saw what they believed at first to be an ostrich sitting on top of a friend's house. The two men called the fire department, which then shot a hose at the Jersey Devil. The water knocked it off the house at first, and it seemed as though it was fleeing, but surprisingly the creature turned and began to charge its tormentors. The crowd began throwing anything they could at it in an attempt to stop it, but nothing seemed to work as the creature barreled headfirst towards them. Finally, before the creature made any contact with the scared onlookers, he spread his wings and soared over their heads into the dark night sky.

- **Camden, NJ**

Mary Sorbinski became the first human to witness a Jersey Devil attack on another living creature. She heard a commotion in her backyard around 7 P.M., and upon remembering that her dog had been out there, immediately went to see the cause of the noise. She was stricken with shock and terror as she saw her dog in the "vise-like grip" of a "horrible monster!" Mrs. Sorbinski then began to smack at the creature with a broomstick, and it dropped her dog and began screaming its awful high-pitched cries. The creature flew right at Mrs. Sorbinski, but at the last second changed direction and flew away. After it had gone, Mrs. Sorbinski carried her injured dog into the house to find that a chunk of its flesh had been ripped out. She became overwhelmed with fear and panic. Within an hour, the house was filled with neighbors, police officers, and others who were curious as to the night's incident. While the crowd gathered, the Jersey Devil made its presence known once more at the Sorbinski residence by emitting its awful screeches. The police officers on scene attempted to fire at the creature, but to no avail. It eventually flew away. This entire incident caused a statewide outbreak of panic and fear.

FRIDAY, JANUARY 22

- **Camden, NJ**

The creature woke the residents of a house with its hoofsteps on their rooftop at 2 A.M. Policeman Louis Strehr observed an eerie creature drinking water from a horse trough at approximately 4 A.M. He said the creature had "the head and body of a kangaroo, antlers like a deer, and bat wings."

- **Mount Ephraim and Gloucester, NJ**

The areas were in sheer panic. Schools were closed, offices shut down, and employees called out sick for the day, afraid to step outside and be exposed to the evils of the Jersey Devil.

- **Chester, PA**

Two girls heard a noise coming from a stopped train. They watched as the Jersey Devil flew out of an open boxcar and took off into the sky.

- **Morrisville, PA**

A report was given that the Jersey Devil had been captured in a man's barn. Upon opening the doors to the barn, the hunters were disappointed to find that the creature had vanished.

- **Trenton and Woodbury, NJ**

The Jersey Devil was seen throughout these areas for brief periods of time.

- **Salem, NJ**

Jacob Henderson saw a beast with "wings and a tail" walking through an area of town. Henderson's bulldog growled and drove the beast into the woods.

1918

In Paterson, a strange creature was killed and exhibited. It was believed to be a possible carcass of the Jersey Devil.

1920

A posse in Salem supposedly treed the Jersey Devil, but nothing more became of this rumor.

1925

A man in Greenwich Township discovered the creature eating chickens. The story goes on to say that the man chased it, shot it, and exhibited the carcass, but this story was never proven.

1927

A cab driver on the way to Salem pulled over to fix a flat tire and saw a creature, which stood upright and was hairy. The creature landed on the roof of the car and shook it, and then flew off.

1930

Two men from Erial saw the Jersey Devil, and later the same day their two daughters also saw it in the same spot it had been in earlier. Berry pickers in Leeds Point and Mays Landing also spotted the creature during this year.

1932

The Jersey Devil was chased in Downingtown, Pennsylvania.

1935

Sighted in Woodstown and described as a big "police dog." Horrible screams were heard throughout the year in Absecon.

1936

More reports from Woodstown—people of the town heard chilling screams and cries. Search parties went out and combed the area but found nothing.

1937

A hunting posse was formed after witnesses near Downingtown, Pennsylvania, reported seeing a strange kangaroo-like creature around dusk on July 28. A full report appears in an undated *Evening Bulletin* article.

1950

A driver reports being chased by a two-legged creature in Lowerbank. The creature kept up with the car until it reached approximately 50 miles an hour, when the beast disappeared.

1951

The Invasion of Gibbstown. A young boy saw a creature looking into the window and was so shocked that he screamed and went into convulsions. The next night, another boy experienced the same thing. Several couples heard unearthly screams, like "wild birds." Several people went out in search of the creature, and one man claimed that "it" almost grabbed him in the woods. Another resident searched and claimed to have seen the creature for an instant before his flashlight blew out. These sightings caused an incident of mass hysteria—people were running through the woods with weapons, ready to fire at anything that moved. Police arrested anyone in the woods and placed signs throughout the region that the Jersey Devil was a hoax. Meanwhile, they found strange, unexplainable tracks.

1952

Strange prints were found, but were proven to be a hoax created by a bear's paw attached to a stick.

1957

Eerie, charred remains were discovered in the woods. It was a partial carcass that included claws, feathers, bones, and hind legs. This carcass was believed to be the end of the Jersey Devil. Officials at the Department of Conservation could not identify the remains.

1959

In Wall Township, a group of boys was fined $50 when they were caught hunting in the woods. The boys claimed to be hunting the Jersey Devil. Also that year, a pair of sisters witnessed the Jersey Devil clinging to their bedroom window in Bridgeton.

1960

Eerie noises were heard and strange tracks were found in Dorothy and May's Landing. Two rewards were announced for the Jersey Devil's capture—one for $10,000 and one for $100,000. Two people heard rustling noises in the bushes in Mullica Hill

1961

Two couples parked in cars heard screeches outside. When they got out of their cars, they found scratches on the roofs. They later saw the creature flying off in the distance.

1963

Five men on a hunting trip at Lake Atsion, near Batsto, found 11-inch tracks and heard loud screams in the woods.

1964

Screeches were heard in Estell Manor.

1966

Mangled dogs and livestock were discovered on the banks of the Mullica River in April. One man found thirty-one ducks, three geese, four cats, and two dogs mangled. One of the dogs was a 90-pound German shepherd whose throat had been ripped out and body dragged a quarter mile from its chain. A state trooper later saw the creature taking livestock and found giant footprints. Unfortunately, the ground was too wet to make plaster casts. Later that year, a girl saw the Jersey Devil heading off into the woods. On September 9, a couple witnessed a glowing horselike creature in Edison. The Rutgers Rarities team investigated this incident.

1969

A man watched the Jersey Devil jumping across the road directly in front of his car in Sweetwater.

1970

The Jersey Devil is blamed for pulling a child's hair in Mercer County.

1971

Mysterious chicken deaths in Leeds Point are thought to be acts of the Jersey Devil.

1973

Several couples witness a large, winged creature fly out of the brush in Manahawkin. Also this year, a young girl outside with her mother and sister hears a horrible scream in the woods of Leeds Point.

1974

An ambulance driver heard screams from within the Pine Barrens. Near Batsto, in the Wharton State Forest, a carful of passengers saw a strange creature cross their path. Also this year, paddlers on Cedar Creek watch a creature following their canoe from the shore.

1975

A horse was found in Williamstown with its throat completely ripped out. Many people believed that it was the handiwork of the Jersey Devil. A group of kids had a possible Jersey Devil encounter. One of the children, years later, would end up telling the story in media accounts. In October, a man witnessed a strange winged creature flying towards him in Somerset. The creature hovered nearby until it took off.

1976

A gas station attendant in Jackson Mills claimed that the Jersey Devil constantly followed him home. Pigs mysteriously died in Pedricktown, sometimes quite violently. Although never witnessed, many believed this to be a Jersey Devil raid. A young man encountered a creature that hissed and screamed at him in Long Branch. In July, a woman witnessed a strange creature walking on the other side of a lake in Batsto.

1977

In January, there was a sighting in Chatsworth. In the summer, a woman said that she saw the Jersey Devil eating blueberries in the Pine Barrens. In Penns Grove, a beast grabbed the door handle of a woman's car and ran alongside at a speed up to 60 miles an hour. Tuckerton also saw its share of activity, as the Jersey Devil made loud noises, dented trailers, and spread footprints all throughout camps in the area. In summer, a woman had an up-close-and-personal encounter with a creature outside her window in Vincentown.

1978

A group of teenagers spot the Jersey Devil in Chatsworth, describing him as having red eyes and a bad odor. In June, two campers in Atsion complained to park rangers that the screams of the Jersey Devil kept them awake all night. Similar howls and screams were heard later that year in Smithville and Chestnut Neck. A boy in Jersey City awoke to find something scratching and screaming outside his window. He screamed and ran into bed. By the time his father arrived, the creature was gone. Two camp counselors locked themselves in a laundry lodge at a YMCA camp in Blairstown after hearing horrific, unidentifiable howling and screaming.

1979

A couple in Tabernacle Township claimed that the Jersey Devil was making horrible cries in the woods behind their home. A few students from Stockton State College in Pomona attempted to track the Jersey Devil after a sighting on campus, but to no avail.

1980

The Jersey Devil made a brief appearance running across a street in New Egypt. During the winter of that year, the Devil allegedly banged on sheds in Waretown nightly.

1981

A young couple saw the Jersey Devil at Atsion Lake. Canoers also claimed to have been followed by a creature moving through the underbrush along the Mullica River.

1983

A couple from Paisley hears screams in the woods. On July 10, a group in the woods in Bayville witness a small horned creature jump from treetop to treetop and disappear in the direction of Cedar Creek.

1984

Jersey Devil screams in Chatsworth became so loud that they were overpowering a chainsaw and forced woodcutters to leave the job.

1985

In the fall of 1985, a creature runs past a window and is witnessed by two boys and their mother in Tabernacle. In December, a creature is seen on the bridge on Ravine Lake Road in Bernardsville.

1986

A woman reported seeing a creature with a long tail standing on a rooftop in South River. Several other witnesses in the car with her also saw the creature and could not identify it. A man reported seeing a winged creature near South Toms River in the summer.

1987

A German shepherd is found 25 feet away from its chain, with its body torn apart and gnawed upon. The dog's body is surrounded by strange tracks. A young girl sees the Jersey Devil while on a class trip in the Pine Barrens. In September, the Jersey Devil is seen running in Wrightstown by two men. In the fall, a strange screaming creature in the woods in Waterford circles several people.

1989

A woman witnessed a strange creature on the side of the road in Holmdel during January. A man heard a loud shriek and turned to see a large winged creature standing before him at Bamber Lake.

1990

A soldier in Fort Dix witnesses a strange creature running past his camp on May 22.

1991

Two hunters in Whiting watched a creature walk across a dirt road. A girl saw a birdlike creature with a horse head, hooves, and wings on March 3 in Burlington. In Erial, a man reports approaching what he believed was a bird, only to find a strange winged creature with a horse-like face that flew away screaming.

1992

A group of off-roaders witness a strange creature cross their path in Chatsworth during the winter. A driver sees a creature on the side of the road near Atlantic City on June 6. A soldier at Fort Dix, the same one from the 1990 incident, encounters the Jersey Devil for a second time on July 16.

1993

A woman in Winslow Township claimed that the Jersey Devil visited her property annually every fall. A couple in a parked car saw something run by them in the dark. A boy at camp watched something walk by on all fours with the head of a camel and the body of a bear, with a long tail dragging behind. A Boy Scout troop saw the creature in June at Wharton State Park. In July, several men encountered a creature in Wall Township during target practice. In September, several dirt bike riders encountered the creature in Forked River. In October, a group of campers witnessed the creature jump across a stream.

1994

A couple in Jackson heard eerie screeches outside their home while in their backyard. The creature circled the two for some time, screeched repeatedly, and left. Later on that year, the couple was outside again and heard the same screeches. Similar sightings were reported, under the same conditions. It is suspected that a bonfire attracted the creature.

A driver watched a strange creature jump out in front of his car near Wildwood in February. In the summer, a boy from Bucks County, Pennsylvania, had a possible Jersey Devil experience. In October, a group of Girl Scouts camping at Bass River State Park is awakened in the middle of the night by screeches. Also in October, a group of boys watch a strange creature that looks like a horse on two legs walk into a cornfield in Millstone.

1995

A strange beast was seen hopping along the side of Route 287 in Pompton Lakes. In December, a woman watched the Jersey Devil sitting along a highway. Strange noises and unidentifiable footprints were reported from Brick.

1996

A driver watched a strange creature follow his car down the road while glaring at him with red eyes. A woman heard noises in Medford Park in July. A driver witnessed a strange pinkish creature about the size of a dog walk across the road in Sparta during the summer. A boy and his friends hiking in Mount Misery witness a creature scream and fly off. On August 8, two Philadelphia police officers witness a strange creature in the woods in Smithville.

1997

A man hiking on the Batona Trail was chased out of the woods by a creature that was no more than 20 feet behind him. In May, a man was awakened in the middle of the night to screams in Wall Township; he looked out the window to witness a creature in his backyard. A Southampton boy woke up to find his dogs going crazy and heard screams in the woods. Another Boy Scout had a strange encounter in the Pine Barrens in the fall. A man reported watching a creature flying in the trees near him in Magnolia in the summer.

1998

In April, a Sussex man saw something in his backyard with glowing red eyes and a horselike or doglike face. In July, a strange creature was spotted one night in Bayville sitting in the road. During the summer, a man at the Hopewell Valley Golf Course encountered a strange animal that flew off screaming; the screams were heard for the next three weeks off and on throughout the nights. In October, a man saw a large creature jump out onto his trail in Leeds Point. A woman witnessed the Jersey Devil shredding and devouring a dog carcass in Leeds Point. A boy and his friend saw the Jersey Devil while walking on a path. A truck driver slammed on his brakes in the Pine Barrens to witness a creature in the road let out a blood-curdling scream before flying off. A boy riding a bike in Old Bridge witnessed a strange gorillalike creature staring at him at the edge of the woods.

1999

A boy camping at Mount Misery heard and witnessed a strange creature on February 17. A teenager saw a strange creature perched in a tree around dusk at Bamber Lake in March.

Campers returned to find their supplies rummaged through after hearing screeches on July 4 in Leeds Point.

In October, an ATV rider is chased out of the woods by a two-legged, hoofed creature making indescribable screams. On October 2, a teenager claimed to have seen the Jersey Devil step out of the woods at Bamber Lake; the creature then flew away.

On October 8, a couple was entertaining guests on their porch in Jacksonville; they began to hear strange noises and saw a glowing object. On October 18, a driver watched something strange cross the highway in front of him on Cape May Avenue in Atlantic County. On October 23, two people hit a mysterious animal with their car in Ramsey; the creature scurried off into the woods. On October 26, a hiking class in the Forked River area discovered strange footprints; the Jersey Devil made a quick cameo when he flew across the path they had been hiking.

A family attempting to make a Jersey Devil video heard screams and witnessed a creature fly past their car in November at Bamber Lake. A class of twenty students witnessed a creature fly over the woods and land in Forked River on November 16. In Stoney Brook, two fishermen heard footsteps approaching behind them and turned to see the Jersey Devil. A boy from Moorestown saw a creature running through the woods on December 3. A couple in Pomona watched something strange in the woods on December 26. Also that day, two girls from Sewell saw something strange in their backyard. While decorating for Christmas, a man in Dover Township hears unearthly screams and witnesses movement in a tree in December. Two hikers are followed through the woods in Westmont.

2000

On January 10, several people in Pennsylvania encounter the Jersey Devil in a park. A young girl sees a creature with "a head like a dog and face like a horse" sitting on a fence in Leeds Point on January 12. On January 16, a couple hears screeches and sees a horselike creature on two legs run past them in Batsto.

On February 1, a man feels "stalked" and sees a creature outside his home in Mays Landing. A series of strange Jersey Devil-related incidents occur between February 4 and 5 in Holmdel. Seven people witnessed the Jersey Devil visiting Philadelphia as he flew overhead on February 24. A pizza deliverer saw and heard a strange creature in the woods in

Great Meadows on February 25. Three men heard something, and witnessed a creature that fit the Jersey Devil's description fly over their heads in Morristown on February 27. The Jersey Devil chased a boy and his dog on April 15 in Toms River. A man and his sisters hear and witness the Jersey Devil near the Bayonne Bridge on April 28. One man watched a creature fly overhead in Paramus on May 11. Two travelers drove past a strange creature perched in the woods in Gibbstown on May 22. A couple encountered the Jersey Devil in Leeds Point on June 23.

An out-of-state cop watched something fly over the trees in Sea Breeze on July 1. Two drivers saw a creature sitting on the side of the Garden State Parkway near Atlantic City on July 2. A girl was approached by the Jersey Devil in Hillsboro on July 7. Five men were chased in their jeep while off-roading in Wharton State Forest on July 17. Two hikers encountered a strange, feathered creature in Leeds Point on October 3.

A college student saw a strange, deerlike creature on the side of the road in Whiting on November 11. Two boys hit a strange creature while driving in New York on December 11. Two girls discovered a strange creature sitting in an abandoned car in the woods in Toms River on December 13. A girl and her friends saw a strange shadow in the woods in Southampton on December 15.

2001

A boy reports strange noises and footprints in Flemington in February. A group of dog walkers witnesses a large creature fly out of the woods in Carneys Point in the spring. A girl hears scraping at her window on April 16 in Burlington. A driver reports seeing something land in front of his car in Newport on April 19. Another driver sees something in Woodbury on May 13. A woman in Estell Manor witnesses a strange creature land on a barn in her yard in July. Two men in a car witness a large winged creature flying overhead on July 21 outside of Atlantic City. A hunter in Woodbury hears something making strange noises outside his tent on August 3.

2002

Sometime this year, a carful of witnesses sees a creature hopping alongside an isolated road in Absecon. On April 20, a strange flying creature circles a driver at night in New Brunswick. Two drivers watch a strange creature hop across the road in Sewell in May. Also during the year, campers in the Pine Barrens see something with a long tail, horselike face, and horns in the middle of a road in the woods. A boy sees a large creature and hears a horrible scream in Jackson in October. A hunter witnesses terrified deer running and sees a strange shadow on October 31 in Collier Mills Wildlife Area. A family witnesses a strange creature in a tree in Pinehurst on November 2. A family hears terrifying screeches throughout the night on December 12 in Tuckerton.

2003

Loud, high-pitched screams were reported in Runnemede on January 11; motion-detector lights in the area seemed to mysteriously turn on throughout the nights as well. Also in January, strange tracks are seen throughout Marlton after an overnight snowfall; the tracks were shaped like little hooves and in some cases, the tracks approached windows, as if the creature had tried to peer inside. Again in January, a family in Browns Mills woke up and found their yard covered with hooflike prints; the trail seemed to climb up into the bed of their truck before it stopped completely.

Screeches are heard and the Jersey Devil is seen in Wanaque on March 8. On March 16, kids playing manhunt in Egg Harbor City heard rustling and witnessed a creature run off in the distance. Campers in Lacey reported hearing an eerie howling and seeing a strange figure on March 26.

Dogs begin to go crazy and loud noises are heard throughout a neighborhood in Bayonne on April 18. Piercing screams are heard in Mountainside on May 1, and residents report a strange creature in the area. A teenager reports hearing weird screeches and rapid movements in the woods in Morris County during the spring. On June 4, two campers witness a strange creature at Paradise Lakes Campground in Batsto.

Workers in a factory witness something fly and land on a nearby building in Swedesboro in July. Also in July, a girl hears screeching noises and watches a creature fly overhead in Manahawkin. Again in July, a paddler on the Bass River watches a deerlike creature with two legs and wings take a drink on the other side of the riverbed.

A couple reports seeing a strange winged shadow fly overhead in Brick on September 5. On September 18, witnesses in a truck feel something hit their vehicle and then watch a creature run past them. In October, a Boy Scout troop hears high-pitched screams in the distance while at a campground in the Pine Barrens. On October 31, a man is chased out of the woods by a creature in Leeds Point.

2004

On February 18, a family in Egg Harbor Township has a strange encounter with a creature that leaves their roof scattered with prints and the police baffled. On March 19, several teenagers witness something flying and land behind a strip mall in Sparta; several screeches and hisses were heard. On June 17, a boy sees a strange creature flying in a weird fashion in Franklinville. During this summer, a girl saw a huge dark creature with wings and horns in the woods of Browns Mills. On August 12, two campers witness a strange, small creature rummaging through their backpacks in the Pine Barrens. On

August 21, a group sees a tall, dark creature on a trail in Batsto; the creature follows them from a distance until they leave the park.

On August 31, a man hears strange, loud screeches in Vernon. On September 1, kids playing in South Plainfield hear a strange screeching noise that seems to follow them as they leave the woods.

On October 1, screeches and unexplained footprints are reported in Pemberton. On October 23, a family traveling through Wharton State Forest witnesses a huge creature flying overhead and landing near a stream; later that night, campers in Paramus witness something in the woods.

On October 26, a woman witnesses a creature fly down and land in a CVS parking lot in Smithville. On October 29, a group sees a strange creature in Leeds Point. On November 3, a strange creature in the Pine Barrens chases two boys. On December 12, a group discovers strange footprints and hears screeches in the distance in Smithville. That same morning, loud screeches are heard in Freehold.

2005

On January 20, a man watched a strange creature flying in Dallas, Georgia. Strange footprints were found the morning after a snowfall in Wallington on February 25. On March 5, a couple was chased out of the woods in Leeds Point by a strange birdlike creature. On April 27, a woman and her husband in Mullica Hill had difficulty sleeping when they were kept awake by strange screeches in their backyard. On June 25, a man watched a large birdlike creature fly by in Wayne.

In August, a man watched a creature fly across the road in Jackson. On August 6, two campers reported hearing a series of high-pitched, unidentifiable screams in the night in Hope. On August 10, a man encountered a strange humanoid figure standing in the middle of the road hunched over a deer carcass in Bass River State Forest. On August 27, campers in Bodine Field, Wharton State Forest heard strange biomechanical screams in the middle of the night. The same day, two travelers trying to fix a flat tire in the Pine Barrens encountered a creature that jumped out of the woods and screamed at them.

In September, a photographer in Pomona was chased out of the woods by a humanlike figure with a horse face and bat wings; the creature screamed and eventually ended the chase. Also in September, a camper witnessed a strange creature approaching her campsite in Bass River State Forest. On October 20, a party in Spotswood witnessed two red eyes walk towards the woods; the creature then jumped on a fence, made a noise, and flew off into the night. On November 5, a woman witnessed a strange creature standing in the woods in Medford Lakes. On November 17, two campers found a creature rummaging through their campsite at night; they fired a shot at the creature and chased it through the woods, where the creature eventually climbed into a tree and took flight. On November 21, two girls saw a strange creature with glowing eyes eating something in the woods in Hopewell. In December, a woman reported that she has been hearing horrific screams in the woods in Randolph. These screams had been ongoing since 2004.

2006

On January 3, two campers report strange, unidentifiable, high-pitched shrieks in Wharton State Forest. On January 21, two girls see an odd creature with wings and glowing red eyes in the woods in Vernon. In March, a driver witnesses a strange hunched creature with a doglike face and kangaroolike body cross the White Horse Pike in Hammonton. On July 2, a woman sees a tall creature with a long neck standing in the shadows at the edge of the road near the Oyster Creek Inn at Leeds Point. On July 11, four people in a backyard in Manalapan see something with large black wings in a tree. On August 27, a man watches a creature fly alongside his car for about a mile in Manchester Township. On September 5, a man hears scraping on his roof and watches a creature fly away in Hamburg. On September 14, a driver witnesses a strange creature fly out of the nearby trees in Port Republic. On October 28, a camper watches a creature on the side of the road in Marmora; at first, the beast looked as if it were a kid in a costume, until the creature jumped across Route 9 and ran into the woods. On November 4, two people see a strange creature in a tree in Rockaway while on a walk with their dogs; the dogs howl and pull them away from the creature quickly, and later they find scratches in the tree and hoofprints in the dirt where the creature had been seen. On December 17, a man observes a bird-like creature flying away after splashing in the water in Pennsville. At some point during this year, a girl sees two strange creatures, one approximately 2 1/2 feet tall, the other 6 feet tall, while walking one night in Voorhees.

2007

In January, a man watched a strange creature fly out of the woods in Mays Landing. A strange creature was witnessed flying into the woods, also in Mays Landing, in February. Several campers in the Burlington area heard strange noises and something large fly out of a tree on April 20. On May 12, campers heard screams and hooves in Califon and eventually encountered a strange creature. On May 20, a man watched a creature with a horse head and bat-like wings walk in front of him in Wharton State Forest. A woman reported hearing high-pitched screams in Leeds Point on May 30. On August 15, a man in Stockholm was dragged by his dog to a tree that held a strange creature. On August 28, a driver watched a strange creature cross Route 542 in Hammonton.

On October 21, a man in Galloway saw a large creature fly out of the trees and continue to shriek as it flew away. On October 27, a hunter in Colliers Mills was chased out of the woods by a creature with a blood-curdling scream. On October 29, a couple witnessed a large, shadowy birdlike creature flying overhead on route 206 in Shamong. The creature dove towards their car and flew off. On November 15, a man watched a skinny, tall creature with wings and hooves fall from a tree in his backyard in Browns Mills.

On December 2, a weird creature with a horse-like face and bat wings was witnessed sitting on a post in a backyard in Collingswood. On December 8, a hunter watched a strange winged creature move erratically through a field in Lawrenceville.

2008

On January 12, campers in the Pine Barrens investigated an eerie scream and caught a glimpse of a strange humanoid creature in the woods. On January 21, a man heard a screech and saw a strange creature perched on top of his chicken coop in Eldora; the large winged animal flew off once the man's cell phone rang. On February 25, a student at Monsignor Donovan High School in Toms River saw a strange winged creature perched on top of a building at dusk. On March 16, a woman driving on the Garden State Parkway near mile marker 19 in Seaville saw a very large creature with red-orange eyes flying out of the woods. Also that same day, a woman saw a gray creature with thin hind legs in the shadows of her backyard in Philadelphia.

On April 1, a driver saw a large creature on the side of the road in the Pine Barrens while driving home that night; the creature flew off as he drove by. On April 13, a woman saw a huge horselike creature with large batlike wings fly through the sky in Jackson. On April 22, a woman watched a 6-foot-tall dark creature hopping alongside the road in Great Meadows. On April 30, a man heard shrieks and saw a strange creature in Toms River. On May 31, a man witnessed a strange creature perched in a tree in his backyard in Wanaque. On June 12, a Sea Isle City man awoke to strange noises and saw an outline of an odd, horned creature outside of his window.

On August 21, a hiker watched a strange creature that resembled an upright horse with wings walking through the marshes in Belleplain State Forest. On September 4, a driver saw something strange flying through the night in Woodstown. On October 1, a strange creature startled a student and his dog in the woods in Jackson.

2009

A hiker heard a strange scream in the air above and witnessed a large flying creature in Mays Landing on January 15. Two canoers saw a strange horselike creature perched on a rock in the Mullica River on January 21. A carful of friends encounters a strange batlike creature hanging from a tree in West Milford on February 7. A creature chased a man into his backyard in the Pine Barrens on February 23; the next day, strange footprints with a four-foot stride between each track were found on the man's rooftop. Strange screeches were heard and a singular hooflike print was found in Mayetta on March 18.

ACKNOWLEDGMENTS

Thanks to the dedicated readers of my *Cryptomundo* blog postings, the fans of my books, and the docents and visitors to my International Cryptozoology Museum in Portland, Maine, for continuing to join me on this ongoing adventure. The process of writing this book came during a time when I lost my mother, several friends, and many research associates. Both of my younger brothers became ill with cancer, heart disease, and other chronic conditions. It has been hard to see death on the doorstep for all these months. I send out my appreciation to my Stackpole Books editor, Kyle Weaver, for his incredible patience in letting my deadlines slip and slip. Perhaps it is the fact the "Devil" is in the mix here, but whereas I used to be early with my assignment due dates, the experience of this book has been an entirely new and difficult one for me. But here it is and I am happy to present it to you.

With regard to the delays, I must also mention my coauthor, Bruce G. Hallenbeck, for agreeing to come on board on such short notice to help me out of a quagmire and then doing yeoman's work with me to get it finished.

Jeff Meuse, the chief docent coordinator at the museum, and his wife Jessica freed up valuable days and much more, so

I could get on with this project. Jennifer Davis, as part of a graduate internship, assisted with compiling some early files for me. My near-New Jersey anomalist books editor and friend, Patrick Huyghe (yes, he really lives in New York), sent me appreciated advice often. Thank you all!

My sons, grandchildren, family, friends, and fans give me insights into our future. Those boys of mine make me quite hopeful.

During the last fifty years of my active cryptozoology pursuits, I have gained inspiration from many quarters. With folks like all of you in my life, supporting me to finish this one, heck, the Jersey Devil be damned (with every Fortean pun intended)!

Loren

I wish to thank Paul Bartholomew, John Carlson, the New York State Library, Robert J. Schneider, and Drew Vics.

Bruce

ABOUT THE AUTHORS

Loren Coleman lives in Portland, Maine, and is the world's leading living cryptozoologist. His first cryptozoology magazine article was published in 1969 when he was twenty-one years old. Since then he has written more than six thousand columns and articles and more than thirty books.

Coleman's cryptozoology columns have included "On the Trail" in the *Fortean Times*, "Coleman's CryptoCorner" in *TAPS Paramagazine*, and "Mysterious World" in *FATE Magazine*. His unique signature column, "The Cryptozoo News," was published in *Strange Magazine* and *Mysteries Magazine* and now appears as his weblog at Cryptomundo.com. His popular books include *Bigfoot! The True Story of Apes in America*, *Mysterious America*, *Mothman and Other Curious Encounters*, *Curious Encounters*, and *The Copycat Effect*.

Coleman established the International Cryptozoology Museum in 2003 and has served as a consultant to several cable television programs, such as Travel Channel's *Weird Travels*, Animal Planet's *Animal X*, NBC-TV's *Unsolved Mysteries*, A & E's *Ancient Mysteries*, History Channel's *MonsterQuest*, and SyFy's *Lost Tapes*.

Bruce G. Hallenbeck is an author, screenwriter, and film director who lives in Valatie, New York. His first book, *Monsters of the Northwoods,* was coauthored with Robert Bartholomew, Paul Bartholomew, and William Brann and published in 1992. The following year, he was a contributing author to the nonfiction book *Dead Zones*. His most recent books are *Comedy-Horror Films: A Chronological History* and *The Hammer Vampire*. Hallenbeck has directed such cult feature films as *Vampyre*, *Fangs*, and *The Drowned*.

Other Titles in the

Monsters Series

Monsters of Pennsylvania
by Patty A. Wilson
978-0-8117-3625-1

Coming in 2011

Monsters of Wisconsin

Monsters of Illinois